JAPANESE FOREIGN INVESTMENTS 1970-1998

JAPANESE FOREIGN INVESTMENTS 1970-1998

PERSPECTIVES AND ANALYSES

DIPAK R. BASU
AND
VICTORIA MIROSHNIK

Routledge
Taylor & Francis Group
LONDON AND NEW YORK

First published 2000 by M.E. Sharpe

Published 2019 by Routledge
2 Park Square, Milton Park, Abingdon, Oxon OX14 4RN
52 Vanderbilt Avenue, New York, NY 10017

Routledge is an imprint of the Taylor & Francis Group, an informa business

Library of Congress Cataloging-in-Publication Data

Basu, Dipak R.
Japanese foreign investments, 1970–1998 : perspectives and analyses. / Dipak R. Basu and Victoria Miroshnik.
p. cm.
Includes bibliographical references and index.
ISBN 0-7656-0502-3 (hardcover : alk. paper)
1. Investments, Japanese. 2. Capital movements. I. Miroshnik, Victoria, 1969– . II. Title.
HG4538.B375 2000 99-23674
332.67'352—DC21 CIP

ISBN 13: 978-0-7656-0502-3 (hbk)

CONTENTS

LIST OF TABLES

LIST OF FIGURES

JAPANESE FOREIGN INVESTMENTS 1970-1998

INTRODUCTION

Various schools of thought have tried to explain international capital flows. The neoclassical school explains the reasons for foreign investments implicitly assuming the positive role of foreign investments and analyzing the role of the large corporations. Nurkse (1972) and earlier authors Heckscher (1950) and Ohlin (1933) have explained the movements of capital in terms of interest rate differentials among different countries. Hymer (1960, 1970) and Kindleberger (1969) have differentiated between portfolio investments and direct investments. According to them, the interest rate differentials can explain portfolio investments but not direct investments. Direct investments are due to efforts of the investors to reduce their risks by having direct control over investment decisions, which they do not have in the case of portfolio investments. Market imperfections cause conflicts and direct investments can reduce those conflicts by minimizing competitions. Several authors, such as Buckley and Casson (1985), Dunning (1972, 1989, 1993), Cowling and Sudgen (1987), have extended this approach.

Akamatsu (1961) has introduced the idea of "The Wild Geese Flying Patterns of Foreign Trade." According to this idea, in the initial stage of development, a country imports goods, technology, and ideas, and starts production to substitute imports. In the mature state of development, the country can start exporting goods. Usually foreign investments follow exports because a firm will try to avoid trade restrictions in a foreign market through direct investments, and, as a result, will compete more effectively by reducing costs of productions using the inexpensive local workforce and/or materials. Japan, for instance, has followed Akamatsu's pattern. Later, South Korea and Taiwan decided to copy the Japanese approach.

Akamatsu's idea was developed further by Vernon (1966) and Hufbauer (1966) in the well-known theory, "Product Cycle Hypothesis." According to this theory, after the initial stage, a new product developed in the

United States or in any developed country will be exported to other developed countries first, and thereafter will be exported to the developing countries.

Thus, as the consumption of this new product grows, it will be beneficial for a company to produce locally in a foreign country and as a result, the technological knowledge or idea about the product will spread to other imitators. After a certain time, the product will be exported back to the country of origin; however, at this stage, it will lose the locational advantages. A number of subsequent theories such as Aliber's (1970), Caves's (1980), and Knickerbocker's (1973) also provide analysis of the determinants of foreign investments.

The latest theories (Ghosal, 1987; Hamel and Prahalad, 1987; Kogut, 1983; Porter, 1990) originating from management literatures have analyzed foreign investments in terms of strategic management. According to these theories, the propensity of multinational corporations to engage in foreign production will be the most pronounced the greater their relative competitive advantages are and the more they find it profitable to create or add value to these advantages from a foreign location.

However, there is an alternative approach (Baran and Sweezy, 1966; Bukharin, 1917; Hobson, 1907) that emphasizes the effects of foreign investments on colonialism and dependent developments. According to this approach, at the turn of the twentieth century, mature capitalist countries suffering from underconsumption as the concentration of production had formed international monopolist capitalist associations that share the world among themselves. The profits from foreign investments are only part of the total profits flowing from the colonies to the advanced countries. Investments in infrastructures are likely to require imports of products from the motherland into the colonies, thus creating extra profits for the manufacturers and exporters. Thus, investments and exports are complementary in this analysis. Baran and Sweezy (1966), for instance, pointed out the recent tendencies among the large corporations to be oligopolist and efficient in reducing costs of production, which lead to increasing surplus, and foreign investments provide one of the channels to utilize these surpluses.

In the following analysis, explanations are provided about capital flows in terms of imbalances in the balance of payments and between savings and investments of various countries. In the modern world, financial capital can flow from one country to another very quickly removing trade restrictions. Thus, the role of international mergers and acquisitions as the route of foreign investments becomes very important. As a result, analysis of international business practices and the behaviors of multinational corporations are very essential in order to explain foreign investments.

Chapter 1 describes the nature and the characteristics of capital flows in the world economy and the specific role of Japan. Also there are analyses of Japan's ties with its major trading partners—the United States and Germany—in order to understand Japan's relationships with the performances of the domestic economies of these countries. Chapter 2 describes the role of various incentives and regulations toward foreign investments on capital flows. There are analyses of a number of surveys conducted among the Japanese companies in order to understand their opinions on various incentives and regulations and in particular how they visualize different countries regarding their comparative attractiveness. Chapter 3 analyses details about Japan's foreign investments such as the geographical spreads, regional importance, and allocations of the foreign investments, and the role of Japanese ventures in each geographical area. Chapter 4 is about the special role of Japan in Asian economic developments through foreign investments. We have described in detail the performances of Japanese foreign establishments, their profitabilities, structures of allocations and networking and in particular the roles of the Japanese subsidiaries on industrial investments in east Asia. Chapter 5 is an extension of the analysis of the previous chapter to analyze the effects of Japanese multinational investments on the Japanese economy. We also analyze electronic industries in Southeast Asia and the role of Japanese foreign investments. Effects of these investments on changes in trade structures of the countries in Southeast Asia and the role of Japan in future developments of industries of that region are analyzed. In Chapter 6, we analyze the economic conditions of the East Asian countries and the effects of the recent economic crisis of Asia on Japanese investments.

Any analysis of Japanese foreign investment is incomplete without describing the role of the Japanese multinational companies, their unique management system, and whether they behave differently in their overseas operations. In Chapter 7, we analyze these issues. Throughout the book there are attempts to assimilate economic analysis and analysis of management systems of modern multinational corporations.

1

RECENT TRENDS IN INTERNATIONAL CAPITAL FLOWS

Capital flows throughout the world in recent years have become more free and flexible than ever before. Immense amounts of capital are flowing between Japan and the United States. Some significant amounts, although much less than the Japan–U.S. flows, are between the developed countries and the developing countries. The economic significance of the later capital flows on the future of the world economy can be even more significant.

In the 1970s, international banks were the most important players in the international capital. Massive amounts of petrodollars were transferred between the oil-producing nations and the borrowing countries during that period. In 1996, net international banks lending was $315 billion, whereas it was only $190 billion in 1995, but now the role of the banks has become smaller than what it was twenty years ago. Although Asian countries are still major borrowers, the direct investments, mergers, and acquisitions are now more important than ever. Recently, portfolio investments in bonds and equities became very important, accounting for more than half of the private sector capital outflows from the developed countries. Official purchases of bonds can be very important at the time of exchange-rate interventions.

All these capital flows are normally very volatile. These are highly sensitive to the changes in the stock markets and changes in the balance of payments of different countries. Some of these flows reflect speculative activities in the foreign exchange markets and stock markets. For example, Japan was running balance of payments surplus; thus, these inflows were not required to finance current account imbalances there. During the first six months of 1996, about U.S.$44 billion flowed into the Japanese equity market with the view that the yen would be weaker than the dollar, and, thus, the Japanese corporate sector would be revived, which did not materialized. In fact, these capital inflows made compensating central bank purchases of U.S. treasury bonds essential in order to stabilize the yen against the dollar.

After World War II, the economic regeneration of Japan was spectacular. Since the 1980s, after gaining special positions and economic maturity through effective utilizations of the world trading system, Japan became a large exporter of investments. Initially, Japanese investments started in order to avoid the tariff walls set up by the European countries, but recently, due to the strengthening of the exchange rate of the yen and continuous improvements of the wage rates in Japan, it is no longer profitable for large Japanese multinational corporations to produce at home. In order to maintain their share in the international market, Japanese corporations are increasingly shifting their production bases to overseas countries with lower wage rates. Following the lead of some large corporations, Japanese medium-size companies as well are moving overseas.

For many years, international investments were nothing but large-scale purchases of U.S. bonds—both treasuries and corporates. These purchases have been linked to the persistent need to finance the U.S. balance of payments deficits of about $150 billion a year. In 1995, these foreign capital flows into the U.S. bond market went up to $220 billion. That was because the investments by Southeast Asian central banks supplemented normal private sector flows after the conversion of the yen to dollars. Central bank intervention is normally due to political motives; however, private sector portfolio investors have specific economic objectives, and in bonds, they seek strength in currency and high yields, whereas in equities, the objective is for diversification and growth.

Bond and equity flows tend to be different. In 1995, there was little foreign buying of U.S. equities in sharp contrast to what was going on in bonds, whereas the recent heavy buying of Japanese equities has not been matched by bond purchases. In 1995, foreigners were big buyers of German bonds, but they have been net sellers of French bonds. That was because French bond yields have been driven down to some unattractive levels due to tax breaks available to the domestic French investors when they buy government bonds through life insurance policies.

Emerging markets show some of the most volatile flows of all. International money of $62 billion boosted the emerging equity markets in 1993, but after setbacks in Hong Kong, Mexico, and elsewhere in East Asia, the flow was reduced to $20 billion by 1995. In 1996, once again, it has reached $40 to $50 billion. Thus, investors who enjoy risk have a lot of scope in China and India along with Eastern Europe. However, success in the emerging market has been damped by economic and political setbacks during 1997 in some of the most important Asian markets such as Korea, Thailand, and Indonesia due to their dire financial difficulties. Vast sums are available to be channeled into attractive opportunities; however, that money is highly sensitive to the least signs of trouble.

Table 1.1 shows the ups and downs of the attractiveness of various countries and regions for these equity flows. The United States, which was not a favorable destination in 1992, became very attractive in 1993 and very unattractive in 1994. Japan has maintained its attractiveness so far. Europe also has maintained its position as well.

Corporate restructuring, particularly in sectors where deregulation or applications of new technologies are increasing competitive pressures, is one of the reasons for the growth in activity. Privatization, spurred by governments under pressure to raise cash in order to reduce fiscal deficits, has been responsible for some of the biggest deals. New demands for capital, coming from the emerging markets that lost access to international markets following the Mexican devaluation of December 1994, help to explain a surge in issuance of depositary receipt programs (paper that trades instead of underlying shares and helps investors avoid problems linked to settlement and custody in most markets).

Investors are responding positively to new international equity issues, partially reflecting the buoyancy of the secondary markets. U.S. institutional investors are continuing to switch their investments away from domestic markets. Also, European investors begin to follow suit. In response, international banks have increased the scale of the resources devoted to the international primary market, which became one of the most profitable investment banking activities. Most of the equities were issued in Europe, followed by the United States, Canada, and Asia. Other areas are lagging far behind.

Foreign Direct Investments

The total stock of foreign direct investments has exceeded $2,700 billion in 1996, double the amounts in 1988 and equal to about 10 percent of world economic output. Worldwide outflows have reached $318 bil-

Table 1.1

Net Cross-Border Equity Flows by Markets (US$ billion)

	1992	1993	1994	1995	1996
United States	–4.1	24.3	1.8	11.2	10.0
Europe	25.5	68.5	29.1	17.0	30.0
Japan	8.9	20.4	45.5	51.1	30.0
Emerging markets	21.2	62.4	39.9	18.7	50.0
Rest of world	2.2	20.7	3.3	2.0	5.0
Total	53.7	196.3	119.6	100.0	125.0

Source: Bank for International Settlements

lion in 1995, a 38 percent increase over 1994. The contributions of these inflows to host economies are becoming increasingly significant. In 1995, they represented 5.5 percent of total gross fixed capital formation, twice the level in the first half of the 1980s. As well as job creation, foreign direct investment brings transfer of technology and management expertise, exports, and the raising of skill levels. That is the reason why the most developing countries are trying to attract foreign investors and multinational companies. International institutions including the World Bank and United Nations Conference on Trade and Development (UNCTAD) are urging developing countries to adopt the kind of liberal, market-based economic strategies likely to create a congenial climate for investment inflows. One of the effects of these developments is the high proportion of international trade, more than a third of the total accounted for by intracompany transactions. The main factor behind this trend is the transnational spread of manufacturing and the development of global production networks.

Figure 1.1 shows direct investment flows in the non-OECD areas. Asia is the biggest beneficiary, followed by Latin America. Other areas of Europe, Africa, and the Middle East were lagging far behind.

The rapid expansion of international trade in services underscores the traditional relationship between trade and investment. However, the geographical impact of foreign direct investments is still uneven. Despite the emergence of fast-growing economies in the developing world, industrialized countries absorbed two-thirds of worldwide inflows in 1995. This was a higher proportion than in 1982, just before the debt crisis of the Latin American countries. Industrialized countries were also the source of most of the outflows.

Figure 1.1 **FDI Inflows in the Non-OECD Area** ($ billion)

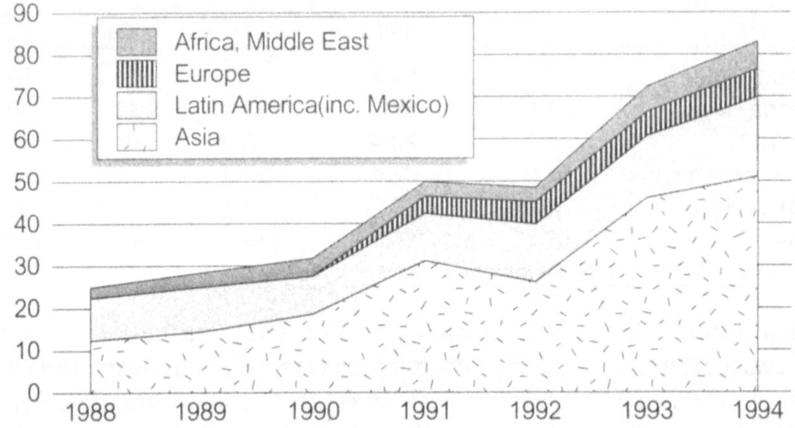

Source: OECD

Imports from the developing world are increasing rapidly and now exceed exports of the developed countries to the developing world. This demonstrates increasing industrialization of the developing world and shifting of production bases to the developing world by multinational companies.

In spite of investments by Hong Kong and Taiwan in China and recent international expansion by South Korea's conglomerates, most developing countries have yet to develop a multinational investment infrastructure. Most Western outflows in 1995 were for mergers and acquisitions. This was particularly true of the United States, which accounted for almost a third of the global outflows. Large acquisition opportunities are much more common in developed than in developing countries. The bulk of foreign direct investments in developing countries goes to about fifteen countries only. For instance, in 1995, China accounted for almost 40 percent of such inflows. Private capital flows into the developing world as a whole overtook official aid some years ago, but they have done little to help most poor countries.

The composition of foreign direct investment flows into developing countries is also strongly biased toward manufacturing. It often reflects undeveloped or heavily protected service sectors. Barriers occur particularly in banking and financial services, especially in Asian countries, which have been reluctant to deregulate financial markets. Malaysia, for example, for many years refused to license new foreign commercial banks. In telecommunications, the need to invest in modern networks created greater opportunities for outsiders. However, many developing countries still impose ownership limits on foreign investors. The persistence of such barriers has increasingly proved a stumbling block to the efforts of the World Trade Organization to liberalize trade in services. The United States has declined to participate in an agreement on financial services on the ground that not enough developing countries were ready to relax curbs on foreign ownership.

Characteristics of International Capital Inflows

The prospect for an increase in international capital flows toward the developing world is bright. Reforms in the way governments and multinational institutions treat very poor nations are helping to ensure that these countries receive more public money and stand a better chance of attracting private sector capital in future.

Table 1.2 shows direct investment outflows during the 1990s. During the 1990s, Japan along with France, the United States, Germany, and the UK are the most important countries regarding international capital flows, and Japan was the foremost country among them. In 1995, Japan was replaced by the United States as the most important contributor. Japan and Germany are not major recipients of direct investments, but the United States, UK, and France, are (Table 1.3). Direct investment outflows of Japan and Germany are due to their domestic factors, that is, high wages, high exchange rates, and balance of payments surplus. For the United States, UK, and France, direct investments are caused by increased competition posed by foreign firms, forcing domestic firms to move abroad to reduce their costs of production and to capture new markets. Several important developments occurred in official financing for developing countries recently. In December 1994, the agreement of the Paris Club of creditor nations allowed up to 67 percent debt reliefs for selected poor countries that have resolved their outstanding debt problems and prepared for reentry into the world financial community and possibly into the capital markets. There are proposals to alleviate a large part of the burden of multilateral debts. The World Bank's proposed Trust Fund and the plan to sell a proportion of the International Monetary Funds (IMF's) gold reserves would be used to finance this objec-

Table 1.2

Outflow of Foreign Investments by Major Countries Based on the Balance of Payments (US$ million)

	1990	1991	1992	1993	1994	1995	1996
United States	29,950	31,380	42,660	77,950	69,260	86,740	87,810
United Kingdom	19,320	16,310	18,990	26,580	33,800	44,090	44,590
Germany	24,200	23,720	19, 670	15,260	17,180	38,530	27,790
Netherlands	15,395	13,567	14,409	12,069	17,306	19,408	21,399
France	34,823	23,932	31,269	20,605	22,801	18,734	26,547
Japan	50,500	31,620	17,390	13,830	18,090	22,510	23,440
World	233,718	193,025	192,150	226,066	262,161	334,231	331,870

Sources: UNCTAD, IMF, and JETRO

Table 1.3

Inflows of FDI in Major Countries Based on the Balance of Payments (US$ million)

	1990	1991	1992	1993	1994	1995	1996
United States	42,920	22,010	17,940	48,990	45,680	67,530	76,960
United Kingdom	32,430	16,210	16,140	15,540	9,180	22,500	32,350
Germany	2,530	4,110	2,640	1,950	1,680	11,960	3,180
Netherlands	12,343	6,337	7,836	8,561	7,356	11,233	7,101
France	13,183	15,153	21,840	20,754	16,628	23,735	20,068
Spain	13,984	12,493	13,276	8,144	9,359	6,118	6,369
China	3,487	4,366	11,156	27,515	33,787	35,849	40,180
Singapore	5,575	4,887	2,204	4,686	8,368	8,210	9,440
Thailand	2,444	2,014	2,113	1,804	1,366	2,068	2,336
Malaysia	2,332	3,998	5,183	5,006	4,342	4,132	5,079
Indonesia	1,093	1,482	1,777	2,004	2,109	4,348	6,194
World	233,718	193,025	192,150	226,066	262,161	334,231	331,870

Sources: UNCTAD, IMF, and JETRO

tive. Such initiatives would not only lessen the burden imposed on poor countries of large debt interest payments, but would also greatly increase the abilities of these countries to attract new capital from private financial markets.

Another important development in official financing was the support for Mexico in early 1995 and the support for the East Asian countries and Brazil in 1998. Subsequent efforts were made to create safeguards to ensure that financial turmoils like that of Mexico and of East Asia are less likely to happen again. These safeguards, such as better financial supervision and data standards, larger emergency credit arrangements and recommendations to ensure a fairer deal for creditors in case of a crisis, represent an attempt to set up a framework of checks and balances in which countries can operate without government interference and more effectively attract sustainable investment flows.

The flow of capital via securities into the developing world has managed to withstand the sharp rise in U.S. long-term interest rates at the beginning of 1996. Rise in the share of foreign direct investment inflows going into countries outside the OECD area increased since the late 1980s. The flow into the developing countries reached about $80 billion in 1994. Deregulations, privatization, and liberalization include dismantling of trade barriers in these countries. They have created an environment more conducive to inward investment.

However, the most important factor is the rapid economic growth in many developing countries. As economies of developing countries grew, the incentive for foreign companies to locate in these growing consumer markets increased significantly.

Japan has invested in a significant way in East Asia. The Asian newly industrializing economies (NIEs, i.e., Korea, Taiwan, Hong Kong, and Singapore) are the most important destinations for Japanese direct investments. For the United States as well, these countries are very important, but Japan is the more important destination for U.S. foreign investments in East Asia. For the European Union (EU) as well, Japan is the more important destination than any other East Asian country. The attractiveness of China is falling for both the United States and Japan, but the EU still considers China attractive. China also receives a lion's share of direct investments from the Asian NIEs.

Rapid globalization of the world economy brings profound changes in manufacturing industry. Companies face ever-increasing international competition and try to take advantage of the growing opportunities offered by the international market. The world economic output grew in the mid-1990s at an average annual rate of 3.7 percent a year; trade increased by more than 8 percent. Trade between the industrialized world and the developing countries grew even faster at more than 11 percent per year. These flows were augmented by the increases in foreign investment in developing countries. Foreign direct investment in the developing countries increased from just U.S.$18 billion in 1990 to U.S.$86 billion in 1995. Thus, manufacturers seeking foreign trade and investment to increase sales and profits try to secure new markets, even in countries that a decade ago offered little prospects, and look for low-cost sources of production, notably in East Asia. These twin motives are driving companies in industrialized nations to add ever more countries to their list of possible locations for trade and profit. For example, in East Asia, coastal China is no longer the pioneering territory. The adventurous companies look inland to cities including Wuhan and Chengdu. Also, recently in Southeast Asia, Thailand became the old area and Vietnam became the new one. In Europe, for instance, despite prospects that Russia is considered a risky area, Poland and the Czech Republic are relatively safe areas for trade and investments.

The sophistication of goods made in the developing countries is rising. Exports from the developing countries now include high-skill goods, including semiconductors, computers, chemicals, aerospace equipments, printing and publishing. These kinds of export rose recently from below $10 billion per year in the late 1970s to more than $40 billion in 1992. For example, exports of medium-skill goods including office equipments excluding computers, machinery, and fabricated metal products rose almost as fast to more than $40 billion. However, exports of low-skill manufactured goods including textile, clothing, and metals rose modestly from more than $40 billion to just under $60 billion over the same period.

An important development is the intragroup trade where companies trade with their own subsidiaries and affiliates. This kind of trade now accounts for 40 percent of world trade in industrial goods. These developments demand changes in the overall management system. Companies now have to build organizations that can respond ever more quickly to a wider range of external changes. It is not enough to have representatives or factories in foreign countries unless these units function effectively, which usually means function quickly. Many large companies are responding to this challenge with a combination of decentralized decision making and rapid reporting of such decisions and their results, especially financial results, to the head office. These policies are often called "global localization." Successful and highly decentralized companies include ABB, the Swiss-Swedish engineering combine; Motorola; and the U.S. electronics group. Less decentralized companies such as General Electric, the U.S. Engineering Group, and the Japanese car maker Toyota are also successful.

Large global companies are mainly from Western Europe, North America, and Japan. Among manufacturing-based groups from the developing world, the South Korean Chaebol Union, Taiwanese, and Hong Kong companies are also the most prominent with well-established operations in the United States and the EU.

Internationalization of large manufacturing of finished goods, including vehicles, electronic equipment, and machinery, poses particular challenges for their suppliers. Often, the finished-goods maker goes to a developing country in search of cheaper component supplies, threatening the business of the domestic component maker. The obvious route is to follow the big customer overseas, but smaller companies are sometimes worried about the costs and risks of establishing themselves overseas. They prefer joint ventures and cooperation agreements with similar-sized suppliers in the foreign country.

There are differences between industries in the degree of globalization. For some industries the cost of transport is a powerful restraint on truly international trade. For example, while steel goods are shipped around the world from Japan to the EU, steel itself is mainly a regionally-traded product. In other industries proximity to the market is crucial. For example, textiles among the earliest manufactures were traded internationally, but domestic manufacturers producing high-fashion items play an important role even in countries with high labor costs because of the speed with which they can reach markets. Thus, globalization is not the solution for all industries.

Current Account in the Balance of Payments and Capital Flows: An Historical Analysis for 1970-1993

Capital Flows and Developed Countries

The total international capital flow observed in the capital account for each country is equal to the current account balance of that country. For the United States, the current account until 1980 was roughly in balance. Since 1983, the United States has serious deficits in balance of payments due to its own budget deficits and very high interest rates, which have caused the dollar to rise against other currencies. On the other hand, the current accounts of both Germany and Japan are in surplus for a long time, although the surplus of the EU countries as a whole have disappeared since 1990. At the same time, the U.S. deficit was re-

Figure 1.2 **Capital Flows by Type and Sector in Asia** (US$ billion)

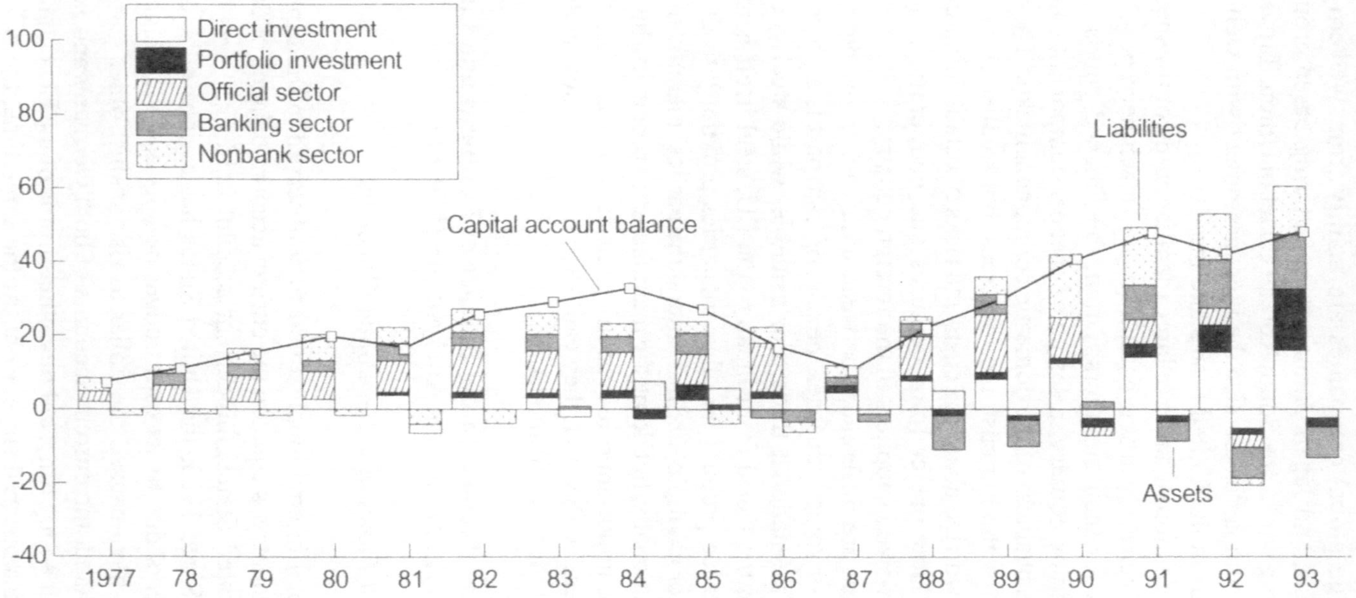

Source: IMF

duced, whereas Japan's surplus rose and rose. The deficit of the United States was reduced in 1991 and 1992 because of the transfer of money from Japan, Saudi Arabia, and Kuwait to pay for U.S. services in the Gulf War; but since 1993, U.S. deficits are rising again. The deficits of the EU countries were reduced and their current accounts are roughly in balance. (See Figure 1.2.)

The United States was the most important source of international capital until 1980. The principal forms of capital flows from the United States since 1970 were direct investment and loans through the banking sector. Since 1980, although the United States became a net importer of direct investments, the banking sector continued to provide outward capital flows. After 1983, because of serious balance of payments deficits, the United States became the net importer of capital in the forms of portfolio investments, bank transfers, and direct investments. Recently, the inflows through the official sector became very important. Most countries use their purchases of U.S. government bonds and dollars to intervene in the foreign currency market in order to stabilize their own currencies.

In Japan until 1981, capital inflows were not so important. Balance of payments imbalances after the oil crises of 1974 and 1979 were financed mainly by inflows through the banking sector and portfolio investments. After 1982, with a large balance of payments surplus, Japan became the net capital exporter; a large part of these were in the form of portfolio investments. After 1988, direct investments became more prominent along with the appreciation of the yen, whereas both capital outflows and portfolio investments have declined due to declining surplus in the balance of payments. After 1991, with an increasing surplus in the current account of the balance of payments, capital outflows have started rising. Whereas there are considerable inflows of portfolio investments, direct investments outflows were reduced.

In the EU, net capital outflows during the 1970s were small due to near balance in the current account. After the second oil crisis of 1979, particularly from 1980 to 1982, the deficits were financed through bank and nonbank borrowing. After 1984, capital exports from the EU became prominent due to surpluses in the balance of payments, with direct investments taking the major role. In the 1990s, direct investments are still prominent although the balance of payments are no longer in surplus. The banking sector became a net exporter, too.

Other developed countries were net importers of capital. During the late 1980s, when deficits in the current accounts became large, capital inflows increased through bank borrowing and portfolio investments. At the same time, direct investment outflows also were increased. During the 1990s, the capital inflows to other industrial countries began to decline. Banks became lenders and thus the portfolio investments became very prominent.

Capital Flows and Developing Countries: 1970-1993

During the first half of the 1970s, the volume of capital inflows to Asia was small and the imbalances in the current accounts were also small. After the mid-1970s, capital inflows became prominent and continued to expand, particularly after 1982, when due to the debt crisis, the Latin American countries were no longer the favorable destinations for foreign capital. The shares of the official borrowings were very high, but gradually the shares of the banking sector and direct investment were rising. In 1986 and 1987, capital inflows declined due to the reductions in the current account deficits; however, direct investment inflows continued to rise. Current account deficits began to increase after 1988 and capital inflows began to rise. The natures of the inflows are now different. The shares of direct investments are higher, the shares of the banking sector and portfolio investments are also prominent, whereas the shares of official borrowing are now declining

For the developing countries, Latin America has had serious balance of payments problems since 1980, the year when the so-called debt crisis started and the large debtor countries were unable to respect their obligations leading to the crisis in the Western banking system. The oil-exporting countries gained since 1973 and obtained some large surplus. However, since 1982, due to the decline in the price of crude petroleum, they have had a reversal of fortune.

In the Latin American countries, due to increased deficits in the current account, capital inflows from the 1970s to early 1980s were very prominent. Another reason was the oversupply of funds in the banking sector of the developed countries due to the deposits made by the oil-producing countries since 1974. Banks were too eager to lend out to the Latin American countries in order to circulate the money, consequences of which were felt since 1982 when Latin American countries were unable to repay even the interest payments. After 1982, capital flows began to decline. The nonbank sector started to export capital, but the official sector was a massive importer of capital through debt rescheduling. There were significant inflows of direct investments. After 1991, capital inflows began to increase again mainly in the form of portfolio investments and direct investments. Due to debt repayments, official sectors have massive capital outflows.

Asian countries have had small deficits throughout these periods; however, recently, their deficits became unsustainable. The oil-exporting countries, from 1974 to 1981, have exported massive amounts of capital from their current account surplus due to increased oil prices. Outflows in the official sectors reflect the aid and investments in the developing Moslem countries; otherwise, mainly portfolio investments to the developed countries were the dominant factors. However, due to the decline in the price of oil since 1993, these oil-exporting countries were experiencing current account deficits, and as a result, they became net capital importers. During the first half of the 1980s, the main forms of capital inflows were portfolio investments and direct investments; later, capital inflows through the nonbank financial sectors were very important. Whereas official sectors were the net exporters of capital for most of these countries, from 1991, large inflows of capital are taking place through the official sector and nonbank financial sectors.

For other developing countries, these deficits were small by international comparisons, but for individual poor developing countries, this period since 1974 was particularly difficult. The oil crisis had caused large current account deficits financed by capital inflows through the official sector and nonbank financial sector. After the debt crisis in 1982, it was very difficult for these countries to borrow in the international markets; thus, capital inflows declined. Since 1992, there were huge increases in capital inflows mainly because of the large-scale capital transfers to East European countries. Capital inflows to Africa were insignificant.

The preceding analysis can be summarized as follows: (a) from the 1970s to the early 1980s, capital inflows were from the developed countries to the nonoil-exporter developing countries; (b) after 1974, the oil exporters were the major exporters of capital; (c) after 1982, capital flows to the developing countries were much reduced, but flows among the developed countries were increased due to imbalances in savings and investments in the developed countries; and (d) after 1987, capital flows among the developed countries were reduced, but direct investments are still dominant forms of capital flows.

Thus, during the 1990s, developing countries became the major recipients of capital inflows. The beneficiaries are mainly the East Asian, Latin American, and some middle-income countries. For the United States, the major importer of capital, the nature of capital flows has changed in recent years. Currently, the important areas of international capital flows to the United States are the official sector and the banking sector. These are due to large-scale purchases of U.S. government bonds by foreign institutions and deposits made by foreigners in U.S. banks.

Causes of Capital Flows: 1970–1993

Characteristics of Savings-Investments Imbalances

In national income accounts, it is very easy to show (Kenen, 1994) that a country's balance of payments will be equal to the savings-investment gap and the public sector balance. If the public sector is in balance, then the savings-investment gap can be identically equal to the balance of payments. With this identical relationship in mind, it is possible to explain much of the capital flows among the United States, Japan, and the EU, and the sources of these savings-investment gaps in these three countries (Tanaka, 1993; Yasuhara, Nishimura, Takada, and Ogawa, 1995).

Japan has a large although declining surplus in the current account and though it has a very low interest rate, the savings rate is very high and higher than that in either the United States or Germany, two other leading countries among the developed nations. The very high rate of investment in Japan fluctuates as well. Thus, the imbalances between rate of savings and rate of investments are due mainly to the fluctuating rate of investments.

In Germany, the rates of savings are very high, but since 1990 they are on a declining path. The rate of investment was always very high and it fell during the early 1980s; thereafter, it remained stable. Thus, the imbalances between the rate of savings and the rate of investments are due to decline in the rate of savings.

In the United States, the current account was in deficit for a long time and savings rates were declining. The absolute magnitude of the rate of savings was very low as well. The United States has a rate of investment that is low and declining. The imbalances between the savings and investments are due mainly to the decline in the rate of savings. During the second half of the 1980s, the investment rate declined as well; thus, savings and investments were balanced, whereas in Japan, the investment rate was rising, which has closed the gap between savings and investments.

In the developing world, the savings rates were high in Asian countries, while the rate of investments continued to grow throughout the 1980s and 1990s. The imbalances in savings and investments were reduced by increased savings. During the 1990s, however, the rates of investments were higher than the rate of savings, which has caused imbalances in savings and investments.

In Latin America, the savings rate during the early 1980s was the same as that in Asia, but it has started to fall. The rate of investment was higher than that in Asia during the early 1980s but went down. Savings and investments were matched during 1980s because of the fall in the rate of investment. Thus, during the 1990s, the imbalances are due to a fall in the savings rate.

The savings rate for the oil-exporting countries was high during the days of oil crisis, but since the mid-1980s it went down sharply. The investment had declined, too. During the 1990s, both saving and investment rose, but there are imbalances due to the lower savings rate than the rate of investments.

Thus, the differences in the savings and investment rates can have implications for the balance of payments. For example, in Japan and in Asia, current account imbalances cause savings-investment imbalances, but these imbalances can be reduced by an increased rate of investment. So, higher economic growth leads to improvements in the balances in both savings-investments and in current accounts. In contrast, in Latin America and the United States the imbalances in saving-investments were caused due to reductions in the rate of savings. The rate of investments is either declining or rising very slowly. Thus, economic growth may not lead to improvements in current account balances, and it may not reduce imbalances between savings and investments.

Characteristics of Capital Flows Since the 1980s

The period from 1980 can be divided into three distinct phases; the period of expansion, the period of contraction, and the period of recovery (Yasuhara et al., 1995). The first period lasted until 1987 for the United States when massive amounts of capital flowed into the country because of its continuous balance of payments deficits where both Japan and Germany were the major contributors.

The forms of these capital flows were mainly direct investments, portfolio investments, and bank lending. German outflows were mainly in the form of portfolio investments. Japanese banks were the major contributors in the capital outflows, and portfolio investments were very important, too.

After the corrections of the overvalued U.S. dollar in 1987, current account imbalances among the developed countries were reduced, and the capital flows between these three countries were reduced, too. Although assets in portfolio investments and direct investments increased, the increase in liabilities was greater in the United States than in Japan or Germany. The overall inflows declined because the banking and the official sectors have substantially reduced capital inflows through reductions in their liabilities.

In Japan, assets in all types of flows went on increasing. In banking and direct investments, changes in liabilities were small; thus, capital outflows were expanded and capital inflows declined. The trends of capital flows in the banking sector and in direct investment were opposite to that of the overall net capital flow. The reduction of overall net outflows during the period between 1986 and 1989 in Japan was mainly due to reductions of outflows or expansions of inflows in portfolio investments and the nonbank private sector. Increases in liabilities were more than the increase in assets.

In Germany in the bank and nonbank private sectors, the increase in liabilities was smaller than the increase in assets; thus, there were increased outflows. The overall reductions in capital outflows were caused by reductions in assets and increases in liabilities of portfolio investments. During 1989 to 1991, current accounts of the developed countries continued to improve and capital flows continued to decline in net and gross terms. Reductions in gross capital flow were large in both assets and liabilities in Japan. In the United States, the reduction was larger for liabilities leading to reductions in inflow. In Germany, it was larger for assets leading to a reduction in outflows.

Liabilities declined for all types in the United States except for the official sector. The portfolio sector has experienced the largest reductions in inflows. There were large reductions in direct investments. In the banking and nonbank private sectors, assets declined. The net reduction was small. In Japan, there were increased assets in the direct investments and official sector. There were corresponding declines in the banking and portfolio sectors. The banking sector became a net exporter of capital as the reduction in liabilities exceeded the reduction in assets. Overall, reduction in outflows was due to expansions of inflows in the nonbank private sector caused by reductions in assets and increased liabilities.

There were reductions in assets also in the German banking sector, portfolio investments, and in the nonbank private sector. Liabilities were increased in the portfolio investments and in the nonbank financial sector. That could have caused outflows. However, because reductions in assets were bigger than increased liabilities, there were net inflows.

Characteristics of Recovery Period from 1991

Recently, current account imbalances among the developed countries increased, and as a result, net capital flows increased, too. In gross terms, both assets and liabilities increased in the United States and in Germany, but in Japan we can observe a reverse picture.

In the United States, there are increased liabilities except for direct investments. In net terms, expansions of inflows are large in the banking sector; there are increased inflows on the asset side. In the official sector and in the nonbank sector, there are slight increases in assets due to expansion of outflows in portfolio investment and in direct investment. In 1993, although the United States has a massive current account deficit, it was also a large creditor in portfolio investments.

Japan, on the other hand, experienced declines in assets except in the portfolio sector. The banking sector became an importer of capital on the assets side but liabilities declined for all types. The bank sector registered a sizable net outflow of capital in 1991 and 1992 with large reductions in liabilities. In the nonbank private sector, reductions in liabilities were greater than reductions in assets. In portfolio investment, assets increased and liabilities declined.

In Germany, the increase in assets exceeded the increase in liabilities in the banking sector and liabilities declined while assets increased in the nonbank private sector, causing the net position to turn to a sizable outflow from an inflow in both types. There was a net expansion of capital inflow because increases in liabilities have exceeded increases in assets in portfolio investments.

During the current phase, assets in both Germany and the United States are increasing; the net inflows of capital are the result of greater increases in liabilities. The principal types of capital flows in the United States are the flows in the banking and the official sector, whereas in Germany the principal type is still in the portfolio investment. Japan's provision of capital has expanded. Now assets and liabilities are both declining. Net outflows now are in the banking sector and in portfolio investments.

The Role of International Mergers and Acquisitions

International mergers and acquisitions (M&As) are some of the most important forms of capital flows recently. They have the obvious advantages of creating market access, local support, and contacts in the host countries. They can take the form of portfolio investment to start with, and then if the new entrant can gain majority holding, direct investment can help to expand the company. In the United States, the share of the foreign investors in mergers is increasing. For example, in 1994, it was 31 percent. In the developed countries, for instance, in 1993, the share of mergers and acquisitions in total foreign investment activities was 74 percent. The volume of such investments in 1992 was U.S.$74 billion. In Europe alone, the U.S. investment in mergers and acquisitions was U.S.$21 billion in 1994.

Japan has played a minor role. Japanese investment in such ventures was only US$2.1 billion in 1994. The most important investor was the United States. European countries as a whole have contributed more in such activities in the United States. Total European investments in mergers in the United States was U.S.$37 billion in 1988 and U.S.$34 billion in 1994. For Japan, the corresponding figures are U.S.$16 billion and U.S.$2 billion, respectively. The major contributor among the European countries in this matter was the UK. Patterns are repeated in the reverse flows as well. U.S. investment in mergers in the UK was U.S.$17.8 billion in 1994, whereas contribution of the United States in Japan was U.S.$853 million. The total U.S. direct investment in 1994 was U.S.$6.2 billion, but total investments through M&As by U.S. corporations was U.S.$35.7 billion.

Another important aspect, which also can enhance stock positions in foreign ventures, is the reinvestment of profits by multinationals. For U.S. companies, the share of reinvestment of profits in 1994 was 69.3 percent, and for the European area, the share was 70 percent. For the Asia-Pacific area, the share was 59.6 per cent in 1994. For all regions, the share went up, whereas for the Asia-Pacific area, it went down. That may signify lesser attractions for Asia for the American companies.

Capital Flows to Developing Countries

The characteristics of capital flows to Asia were different in the 1990s compared to that in 1970s and the early 1980s. During the previous period, the share of the official sector in capital flows was greater. During the later period, the share of direct investment was the most prominent. During the later period, Asian countries were also exporting capitals; as a result, their assets were increasing along with increased liabilities. The net inflow of capital was because liabilities were greater than assets. In the Asian NIEs, the share of inflows into the official sector was low and the share of the private sector was high.

For Asia, capital inflows were in terms of increased liabilities. The official sector had experienced net outflows of capital, mainly due to large-scale amortization of foreign debts. The nonbank sector has also experienced net outflows because its increased assets are more than its increased liabilities. The principal types of capital flows were portfolio investments and direct investments. Currently, although they are still net importers of capital, Asian NIEs are also important sources of foreign investments.

For the ASEAN (Association of South East Asian Nations) during the previous period, the share of the official sector was high as they were in a less advanced stage of development compared to the Asian NIEs. Recently, the ASEAN countries have net inflows of capital and experience current account deficits. The share of the official sector is large. The share of the private sector, mainly direct investments, and the nonbanking sector are gaining more importance. The asset positions are small, and capital inflows are in the form of increased liabilities.

In Latin America during the previous period, capital inflows into the nonbank sector and the banking sector were prominent. Currently, there are significant increases in direct investments and portfolio investments. The increases in gross assets are more or less the same in size compared to those during the previous period. These countries are not sources of foreign investments yet. The most important types of portfolio investments are debt securities as public and corporate bonds.

In Asia, on the other hand, the shares of direct investments and equity securities in portfolio investments are more important. Latin America has serious imbalances between savings and investments and some declining magnitudes of capital exports. The principal type of capital inflow is debt instruments, which shows the weakness in the structure of capital flows.

Considering geographical distribution, the share of private capital flow was dominant during the earlier period for some Latin American countries (Argentina, Brazil, Chile, Mexico). In Asia, equity dominates the scene, showing the importance of short-term equity investments, whereas public bonds from official sources dominate in Latin America. Although during the early 1990s, ASEAN4 was the most attractive destination among these three regions, Latin America is now the most attractive and Central Europe is gaining importance and can be the most attractive region very soon. The share of private capital flow was high in the Asian NIEs, which was comparable to the share of public capital flows in the ASEAN countries. However, in recent years, a slight net outflow was there in the public funds for the Asian NIEs and the share of private funds rose considerably. For the ASEAN countries, the share of public funds is still as important as private funds. In Latin America, the share of public funds went up, whereas the share of private funds declined.

International organizations were the most important contributors of public funds. The United States has the major role for the Asian NIEs and Latin America, whereas Japan and the EU have the major roles in the ASEAN area during the earlier period. Currently, the ASEAN countries are dependent on Japan, whereas Latin America depends on the EU. The importance of the United States has declined in Latin America in the meantime. Regarding private funds, during the earlier period, the share of the EU was prominent for the Asian NIEs. That was also true of Japan for the ASEAN countries and of the United States for Latin America. Currently, the share of Japan in private capital flows is more than 50 percent for both the ASEAN and Asian NIEs; thus, Japan has the most prominent role as the supplier of capital in Asia. Japan, for instance, withdrew funds from Latin America. However, the United States and other developed countries are still supplying most of the private funds to Latin America.

In Singapore and Hong Kong, the shares of public funds were extremely low. Thus, in recent years, the shares of private funds are even more dominant. In Taiwan and Korea in the earlier decade, the shares of public funds were dominant. Currently, flows of public funds are either negative or negligible. Korea has received large flows of private funds. Taiwan has experienced net outflows of private funds, reflecting Taiwan's large-scale involvements in China. During the earlier decade, the share of international organizations in public capital flows was most prominent in Korea. The United States and Japan made significant contributions as well. In Taiwan, the U.S. share was most dominant. During the previous decade, the share of the EU (particularly the UK) was most important for Hong Kong; similarly, the share of Japan was high for Taiwan. For Singapore and Korea, the shares of Japan, the United States, and the EU were comparable. However, during recent years, the share of Japan rose for Hong Kong and that of the EU went down. For Taiwan, the United States withdrew large amount of funds and inflows from Japan and the EU were small. For Singapore and Korea, the share of the United States went on increasing.

Thus, in the ASEAN, the shares of private funds were prominent during the previous decade. The trend was maintained during recent years. In Thailand, although the shares of public funds were important during the previous period, recently, it has experienced some large flows of private funds. In contrast, the shares of public funds are increasing in Indonesia and the Philippines.

Among suppliers of public funds, the share of international organizations was dominant during the previous decade, followed by the EU for Indonesia and Japan for others. Recently, the share of international organizations declined, with inflows from Japan becoming the most important source of funds. In Thailand, there was a net outflow to the international organizations. In both the current and previous decades, inflows from the EU exceeded inflows from the United States.

Regarding private capital, the share of Japan was most important during the previous decade. For Indonesia and for Malaysia, the share of the United States was the most important. For Thailand and the Philippines, the shares of Japan, the United States, and the EU were comparable. However, during the recent decade, Japan's role was enhanced. For the Philippines, Japan alone is supplying funds, whereas the United States, the EU, and other developed countries all withdrew funds in net terms. The share of the United States has declined in all countries in this region except for Indonesia.

Among the suppliers, the combined share of international organizations was largest in public capital flows for all recipient countries during the previous decade. It was followed by the share of the United States for Mexico and that of the EU for Argentina and Brazil. Except for Mexico, Japan's share was small. During the current decade, although the shares of international organizations are still very high for Chile and Mexico, the share of the EU is very important for Argentina and Brazil. Regarding private capital, the share of inflow from the United States was largest for all countries during the previous decade, followed by the EU, whereas the share of Japan was very small.

Regarding public capital, Korea and Taiwan had very strong relationships with the United States; similarly, the ASEAN had a strong link with Japan. In all these countries, the relationships were stronger with both Japan and the United States compared to that with the international organization. The degree of linkage with Japan is now enhanced in Thailand, Malaysia, and Indonesia, but declined in the Philippines. The degree of linkage with the EU remains small except for Indonesia during the previous decade and Thailand during the current period. The relationships with international organizations were greater than average in the previous decade; it has declined until 1997; thereafter, it has enhanced due to the financial turmoils in the East Asian countries.

In Latin America, Mexico's link with the United States is very close, and in the future, it will be closer due to the regional trade pact. The link with the EU is also close. Brazil and Argentina also have a close relationship with the EU. With international organizations, the relationship of Latin America is above average, although with Argentina, it has declined recently. The link with Japan is still not that close.

Thus, in the future, with the recovery of the industrialized and ASEAN countries, demand for capital will be high. The capacity for these countries to export capital will decline.

In the developing countries as well, the demand for capital will be high, particularly in the infrastructure sector. In this situation, fiscal balances of the developed countries should be enhanced otherwise imbalances between savings and investment will increase, leading to higher interest rates worldwide.

Recent Crisis in Japan and East Asia

Foreign investments originating from Japan have been falling since 1996 as a reaction to the decline in Japan's economic growth and the rapidly developing depression that now has engulfed its entire economy. The crisis started first with the collapse of the "bubble economy" created in Japan during the late 1980s with excessive credit expansion by the banking sector. Since the early 1990s, problems of the nonperforming loans were becoming larger and larger and have reduced the ability of the banking sector to expand credit. The resulting reduction of domestic investments has provoked Japanese industries, particularly in the medium and small-scale sector, to invest in foreign locations to avoid the depression in the domestic economy. However, the economic depression in Japan also has reduced imports of Japan, mainly imports from Southeast and East Asian countries that are the major recipients of Japanese foreign investments.

The reduction of Japanese imports from the East Asian countries has started economic decline in those countries; this was further worsened by the rapid devaluation of currency by China in 1994 and the failure of the East Asian countries to respond to the growing price-competitiveness of Chinese exports.

Japan's economy had a growth of –0.7 percent in fiscal year 1997. The negative growth was caused by a sharp drop in consumption and housing demands, and a reduction in public investments. Since 1995, the exchange rate of the yen against the dollar was falling; as a result, exports grew and imports declined. However, the rate of growth of exports was higher than the rate of decline in imports. As a result, the balance of payments surplus of Japan grew as well, which has hidden the real contractions of the domestic economy that was badly affected by the economic crisis in East Asia. In 1998, exports to the Asian NIEs and the ASEAN4 were reduced by 18.6 and 38.4 percent, respectively. Exports to South Korea were reduced by 43.5 percent, to Indonesia by 57.2 percent, and to Thailand by 42.2 percent. In 1998, the sectors mostly affected were electronic parts and semiconductors (declined by 14 percent), computers and office machinery (declined by 12 percent), electronic parts (declined by 18 percent to Asian NIEs), automobiles (declined by 91 percent to ASEAN4). Decline in exports to the Asian countries was compensated by increased exports to Europe and the United States. In 1998, imports from Asian NIEs fell by 19 percent and from ASEAN4 by 23 percent. Almost all categories of imports were affected. In 1998, imports of manufactured products from the Asian NIEs were reduced by 17 percent, from ASEAN by 20 percent, and from China by 7 percent. However, Japanese exports fell faster than imports from the Asian countries; as a result, Japan's trade surplus with Asian NIEs shrank and with ASEAN4 it has become a deficit.

Free movement of capital has often been a driving force behind economic growth in developing countries. However, a great leap in financial technological development has enabled international investors to invest at ease and with great speed. When investors are making decisions in haste and with imperfect and asymmetrical information, free movements of capital may not provide optimum allocations of resources. Excessive capital inflows can lead to overheating of an economy, including increases in unproductive investments, asset-price bubble, inflation, currency appreciation, and reduced international competitiveness and deficits in balance of payments. When outflows start, torrents of outgoing funds could ruin the economy, making the balance of payments unviable. East Asian countries have experienced all these in recent years in excessive amounts.

After the collapse of the fixed-exchange-rate regimes in 1972, it was hoped that a flexible exchange rate would protect the economy from external shocks, including high inflation overseas through automatic adjustments in the current account of the balance of payments. These objectives were not achieved fully; on the contrary, we have experienced volatility and misalignments with large fluctuations in exchange rates, which could not reduce large imbalances among major economies. As the movements of capital have increased in size and frequency, the fluctuations in exchange rates have become even greater, resulting in serious ups and downs in the real economy. The violent effects of these large volumes of short-term capital flows are more prominent in smaller economies like those in East Asia. It has become apparent that these economies will face risks of default due to difficulty in rolling over foreign currency loans or by sudden withdrawal of foreign investments even if they adopt a fully flexible exchange-rate regime. It is often argued that exchange-rate stability would be better achieved through efforts by individual countries toward sustainable low inflation growth for which low fiscal deficits are essential. The question remains whether this is sufficient or whether it can create bad aftereffects by causing a crisis of liquidity in the domestic economy, which can intensify the problem. The apparent failure of the IMF supported adjustment programs in East Asian countries has prompted that reaction from many quarters including the World Bank.

The recent experiences in Asia have revealed the risks of pegging a country's currency to a single currency. Doing that often causes disregard of exchange risks by foreign investors as well as domestic borrowers and sustained misalignment of exchange-rate level with economic fundamentals and consequently leads to a bubble economy that later bursts. Asian countries attracted $28.8 billion of net private capital inflows in 1996; in 1997, there was a net outflow of $44.3 billion. No country can survive these types of onslaughts. Asian countries' access to capital markets has all but disappeared.

Crises of liquidity caused sudden outflows of investments and demanded injections of fresh liquidity in the economic system. That would provide the economy with breathing space that could be used to calm the market and would mitigate panic among overseas creditors. Japan is doing just that by injecting public funds to create capital bases in the banking sector, which are badly affected by the nonperforming loans, which are partly due to the loss of markets for Japanese exporters in East Asia. The economic revival of Japan will promote increased imports from East Asian economies. At the same time, Japan is providing a package of economic aid worth about $30 billion toward these countries, to create liquidities in those economies. Japanese companies are particularly exposed in East Asia, because of their large direct investments in that region. Revivals of these economies are crucial to revive the fortunes of the Japanese corporate sector.

Recent turmoils in the Asian economy along with continuous economic recessions in Japan have their consequences for international capital flows. The Japanese economy after the collapse of the bubble economy of the late 1980s is characterized by an insolvent banking sector. The result is a credit shortage despite an almost zero nominal rate of interest. The government has tried to stimulate the economy by fiscal measures, but has so far failed to have a sustained growth. Due to low rates of profits in the home economy, during the 1990s, Japanese banks have been lending in a massive way to the economies of Southeast Asia (Figure 1.3). The result is an overexposure for the Japanese Banks to those economies. The economies of Southeast Asia also have misallocated their resources by supporting speculative activities in the property sector, and, as a result, local banks are also suffering from severe amounts of nonperforming loans (Figure 1.4). Until 1997, these economies have borrowed heavily from the international financial markets, mainly in the form of short-term loans (Figure 1.5). Due to the growing burden of foreign loans along with declining rates of exports, these economies, particularly Thailand and Indonesia, have started suffering from huge deficits in current accounts of their balance of payments. Then came the speculative attacks from the international currency market. The result was near collapse of exchange rates of their currencies. Figure 1.6 shows the dramatic events during the last half of 1997. Part of the reason why these economies have collapsed so easily was due to the convertibility of capital accounts of their balance of payments, where it was possible for the foreign institutional investor to withdraw portfolio investments very quickly. A comparison with India can help. India has not suffered from these events, as its capital account of the balance of payments is not convertible and its level of deficits in the current accounts and the

Figure 1.3 **Japanese Bank Lending in Asia** (US$ billion; end of 1997)

Source: Bank of International Settlements

level of foreign borrowings are low compared to those in Thailand and Indonesia (Figure 1.7). The short-run prospects for these economies of Southeast Asia are not bright. Effects are being felt in all major economies, but the negative effects for Japan are quite serious because of Japan's very large share of trade and investments with these economies.

Japan's prolonged recession has exposed a dualistic structure in its economy. In the vehicle, electronics, and machine tool industries, where export markets are all important, Japan is still the leader of the world. At the same time, other industries in Japan are still protected from international competition. Without radical restructuring, their future can be in doubt. Despite serious domestic economic difficulties, exports, mainly of the three leading sectors previously mentioned, are still gaining ground in world markets. A recent survey conducted by UNCTAD shows that Japa-

Figure 1.4 Loans to Property Sector and Its Costs, 1997

Loans to the property sector
as a share of total loans
%

Potential cost to economies of non-performing loans
as a % of GDP(%)

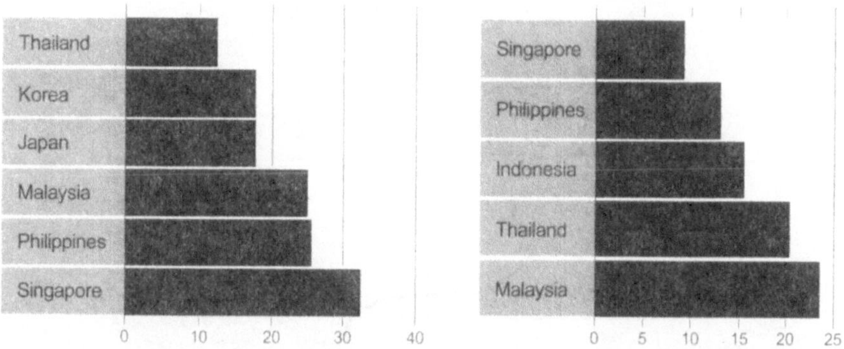

Source: Economic Planning Agency, Japan

Figure 1.5 **FDI Flows, Total Foreign Portfolio Investment Flows, Foreign Portfolio Flows, and Foreign Bank Lending to the Asian Countries Most Affected by the Financial Crises, 1994–1997** (US$ billion)

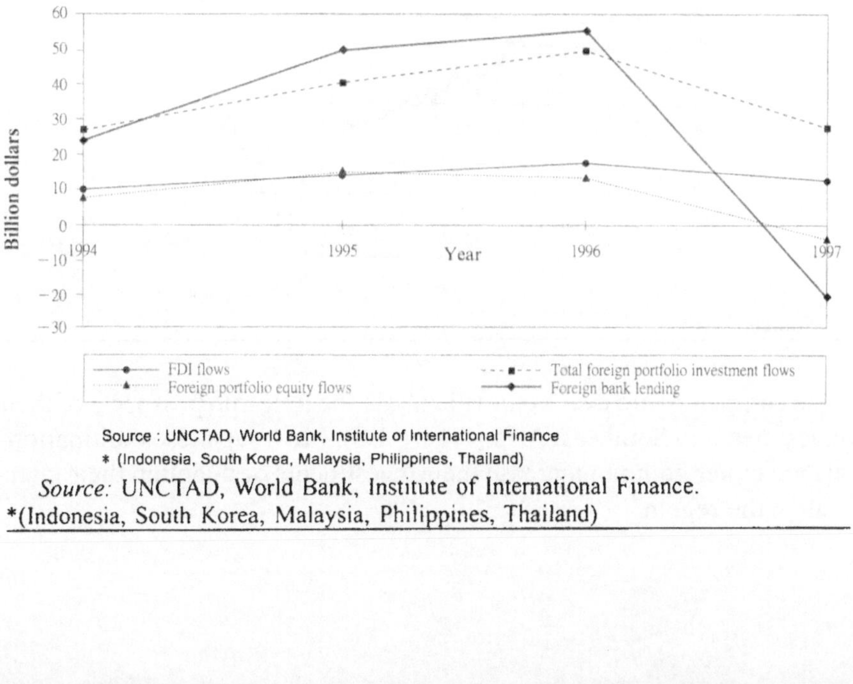

Source: UNCTAD, World Bank, Institute of International Finance.
*(Indonesia, South Korea, Malaysia, Philippines, Thailand)

Figure 1.6 **Asian Currency Turmoils**

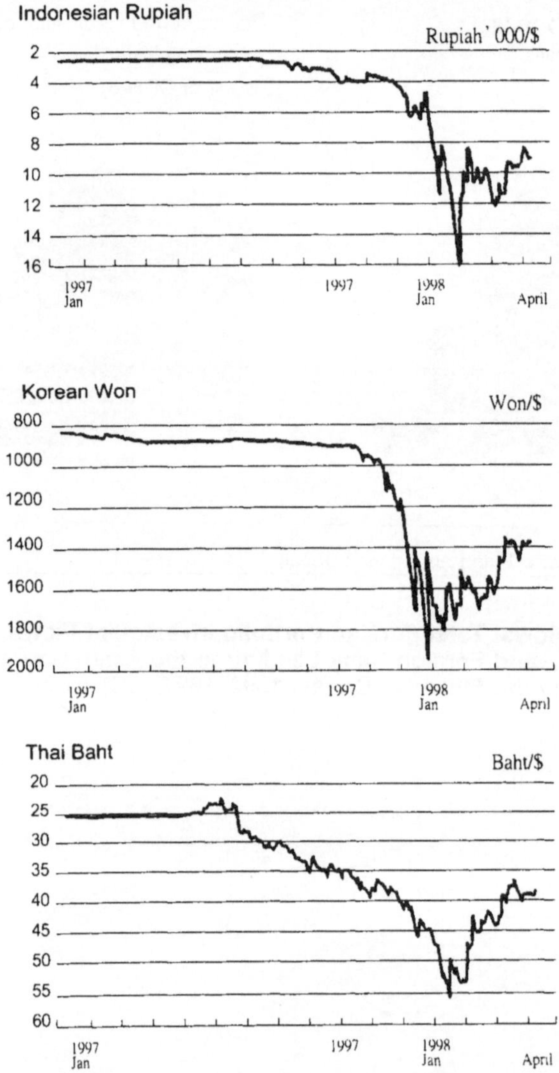

Source: IMF

nese companies are ever optimistic about the long-run prospects of their investments in Southeast Asia (Figure 1.8). Most Japanese multinationals are either going to increase their investments or maintain their interests in the region.

Figure 1.7 **Current Accounts and External Debts: India, Indonesia, and Thailand**

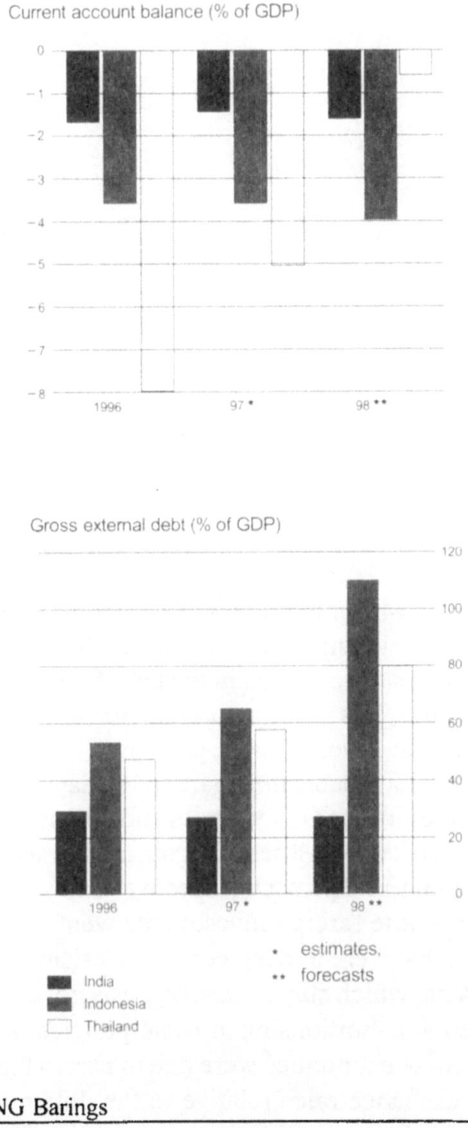

Source: IMF, ING Barings

As Japanese foreign investments follow exports, capital outflows from Japan are still very strong. A moderate decline in investment in East Asia will be compensated by increases in investment in North America, particularly in view of the buoyant U.S. economy. Total Japanese foreign invest-

Figure 1.8 **UNCTAD Survey of Company Intentions on Asian Financial Crisis, 1998**

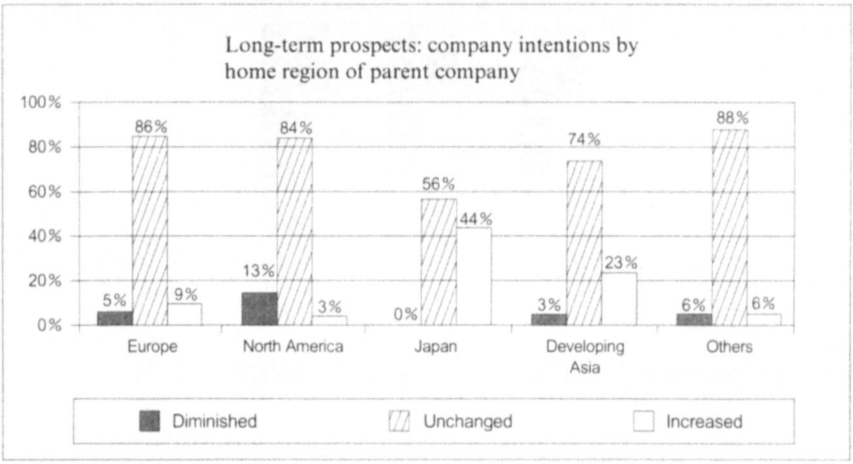

Source: UNCTAD

ment in 1997 reached ¥4,011 billion compared with ¥3,108 billion in 1989. This enlarged foreign investment is changing the shape of manufacturing in Japan. Whereas overseas production in the late 1980s was less than half of the exports from Japan, it is now approaching the level of exports and will soon exceed exports. In 1996, some 9.6 percent of total manufacturing output was overseas output, double the figure for the late 1980s. Although the corresponding figures for the United States and Germany are much higher, about 20 percent, two key industries of Japan, motors and electronics, have high ratios of 20.6 and 16.8 percent, respectively.

The bulk of Japanese foreign investments went to Asia, particularly to those countries that were in deep economic crisis. However, the economic crisis of Asia, which started in 1997, was not caused by a sudden shift in fundamental conditions or in basic policies. Large current account deficits of these economies were due in part to their inappropriate policy of fixing exchange rates relative to the dollar, which has made the exportable from these countries less competitive. Korea is in trouble because its banks and finance companies borrowed too much in foreign currencies with short maturities, thereby accumulating much more short-term foreign debt than foreign reserves it had. However, the IMF insisted on fundamental structural changes in those economies, particularly regarding capital market, labor standards, and government regulations.

The absence of a mature, well-regulated bond market has left banks as the main source of finance for most corporate borrowers, a situation that helped to inflate the asset bubble that has now burst. Bond markets could have helped to allocate Asian savings more efficiently in two ways. They would have given borrowers an alternative source of finance, making the financial system as a whole less dependent on the discretionary decisions of bankers. Also, it might have provided an early warning that assets were being overpriced.

Currently, much of the domestic bond market that does exist is composed of effectively short-term syndicated loans, whereby the bank syndicate buys the debt and holds it to maturity. Because there is no alternative, national savings were mobilized by a selected group of banks. The result is inefficient allocations of financial resources. The economic crisis can now act as a catalyst for change. Most Asian countries are now opening up their bond markets to international investors.

Japan is also going to have some extensive financial reforms. Given these changing scenarios, what would be the future direction of Japanese foreign investments? We think Japan will consolidate its investments in Asia, making investments in proven sectors in safe countries. At the same time, due to its massive involvements in Asian economies, Japan will support more the economic revival of the Asian countries. However, in the short term, it is possible that Japanese investment will be attracted more toward Latin America, North America, and Europe. Given the demands of the major economic partners of Japan for deregulation and liberalization of Japan's domestic economy, it is expected that Japan will be involved more closely in global economic affairs.

2

GOVERNMENT ATTITUDES AND ENVIRONMENTS FOR FOREIGN INVESTMENTS

Most governments now welcome foreign investments, but most also want to regulate them out of fear of losing their national controls over the behaviors of the foreign companies who may go beyond the limits of pure business and can affect the sovereignty of the nations. Through regulations, the host governments want to maximize the benefits they may receive from foreign investments; however, at the same time, they deter further investments by these regulations. Although maintaining the ownership within the country is one of the main ideas of the regulatory frameworks, since the late 1980s, there is a liberalization tendency across the world under pressure of the Western powers and the major international institutions like the World Bank and the International Monetary Fund. Changes in the policy regimes involve changing a number of areas that can be categorized as follows (see UNCTC, 1991):

1. Ownership policies
2. Taxes/subsidies (including tariffs and transfer payments)
3. Convertibility of currency (including limits on dividends, royalties, and fees)
4. Price controls
5. Performance requirements (such as export, local content, and foreign exchange balancing mandates)
6. Sector-specific incentives and limitations
7. Miscellaneous application and entry procedures

The preceding categories cover most of the major variations of government's foreign-investment policies.

Ownership Policies

Ownership policies imply restrictions on foreign-equity ownerships. Such regulations are there explicitly in China, India, Mexico, and several other developing countries, and implicitly in various developed countries, such as Japan, Australia, Portugal, and Spain. Recently, most countries are trying to induce foreign companies to invest by relaxing these restrictions.

Taxation/Subsidies

There are a number of taxes on foreign operations, such as corporate income taxes and withholding taxes, and several subsidies, such as tax holidays, accelerated depreciation schedules, and investment allowances. There are subsidies also in the form of capital grants. An example is the grant of up to 17 percent of the capital cost of a project in "depressed" regions of the European Union. Similarly, a number of developing countries are now offering exemptions from sales tax, or free land or electricity for a specific period.

Convertibility of Foreign Exchange and Remittance of Earnings

Convertibility of local currency into foreign exchange occurs for the import of capital goods for recurrent inputs needed by the enterprise and for the remittance of dividends, royalties, and other fees out of the country. There may be restrictions on the payments on dividends, royalties, and other fees to foreign clients and suppliers. A number of countries have recently relaxed restrictions on capital repatriation. This was done in order to attract foreign direct investment because a nation may be perceived to be an unattractive investment location, despite offering incentives and having few other constraints, if it maintains a tight foreign-exchange regime.

Price Controls

Investors are normally concerned about the future inflations in a host country because that may change completely their calculations regarding future profitability and timing of the projects. Price stability is one of the factors they look for, although future inflation can increase their profitability at the same time by increasing the prices of the products that are already produced. Most governments are trying to reduce their fiscal deficits as an inducement for foreign investors to show the determinations of the government to control inflation.

Performance Requirements

These are restrictions like minimum export commitments and local-content requirements. The host governments can also affect the nature of the technology to be used as an attempt to restrict the unemployment-generating (i.e. labor- saving) production techniques. The export requirements are very prominent features in China, and as a result, most multinationals are using China as an export base with about 70 to 80 percent of their products being exported from China. The local-content restrictions also promote domestic investments. In order to gain access to the restricted market of the EU, foreign companies have made huge investments in the EU. At the same time, the restrictions of local content have forced them to look for local suppliers within the EU, which has created a large number of ancillary industries. However, for the developing countries, these restrictions can deter foreign investments as they cannot provide a profitable market like the EU or the signatories of NAFTA.

Sector-Specific Limitations and Incentives

In developed countries, there are extensive restrictions on the extent of foreign ownership, such as the fishing industries in Finland and the milling of flour in Ireland. Mainly, there are restrictions on broadcasting, transportation, electronics, banking, insurance, and other services. Limitations are placed also indirectly via licensing and citizenship requirements. However, most developing countries are under severe pressure to remove these restrictions on foreign investments, and because of their limited financial means, they are now obliged to do so.

Miscellaneous/Entry and Procedural Rules

Prior authorization for all inward foreign investments are required in most countries whether developed or developing. However, to attract foreign investments, most developing countries are now removing restrictions like these for foreign investments of minority ownerships of

Table 2.1

Effect of Foreign Direct Investment Policy Variables on Different Types of Investments

Market protection orientation	OW	TA	CO	LE	PE	MI	SE	Level
Domestic market	H	U	H	H	H	H	H	
Export market	L	L	U	U	L	H	U	L

Abreviations: H = highly significant; L = less significant; and U = unimportant.
Note: For a full explanation, see Figure 2.1.
Source: UNCTAD.

equities. Meanwhile, countries that have received substantial foreign investments in recent years, such as China and Indonesia, are putting up bureaucratic restrictions on foreign investments in certain areas.

Table 2.1 provides the impacts of foreign-investment policies on investors. In Figure 2.1, the impacts of policies on different stages of productions of foreign enterprises are presented. A distinction is made between domestic and export sales, between imported and domestically incurred costs, and between the entry stage and subsequent operations. Ownership policies affect a foreign investor's cost of capital and the subsequent division of profits between local and foreign owners. In the case of foreign operators using the host country as an export base and selling outside the country through a marketing channel controlled by multinational corporations, the ownership issue is not important. This is because a multinational corporation through transfer pricing may make most of its profits outside the nation. The tax/subsidy category in Figure 2.1 shows that a capital grant affects the entry stage and corporate tax provisions affect a multinational company's repatriated profits after local taxes, whereas subsidies on imported inputs affect the entire enterprise's costs. Usually, tax incentives are not very important in the mind of the investors; this is recorded as unimportant in Table 2.1. Fiscal incentives in the form of capital grants or subsidized inputs are likely to affèct export-oriented investors partially. Convertibility of foreign exchange, price controls, and performance requirements are likely to affect primarily local-market-oriented investors. Similarly, to the extent that much of the output as well as the input of an enterprise are priced in

Figure 2.1 **Which Policies Affect Which Stages of Operations**

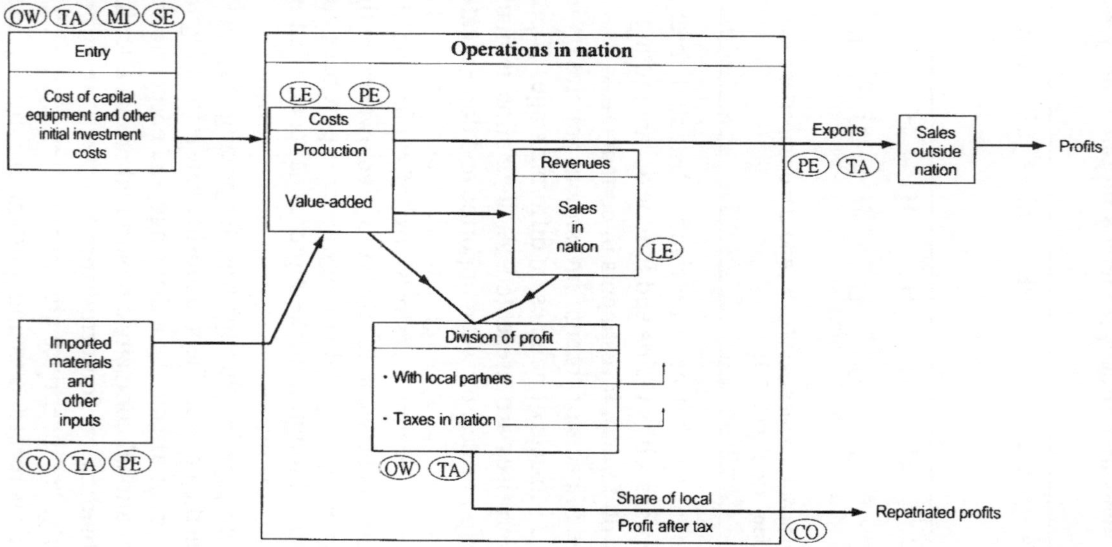

key: → Arrows include financial and non-financial flows.
(OW) = Ownership policies.
(TA) = Tax subsidy transfer payment policies.
(CO) = Convertability of foreign exchange.
(LE) = Price controls.
(PE) = Performance requirements.
(MI) = Miscellaneous: application and procedures.
(SE) = Sector-specific controls.

Source: UNCTAD

foreign as opposed to local currency price controls imposed by the government may not be important.

Global Environment and Japanese Multinationals

The question is how Japanese multinational corporations evaluate different countries regarding their attractiveness and what factors affect them most. Among the Japanese corporations, a consensus has been reached on countries that are considered promising for medium-term or long-term investment. China and ASEAN (i.e., Thailand, Malaysia, Indonesia, and the Philippines, only) continue to attract considerable attention; however, the attractiveness of China is declining. This is due to China's recent policies regarding foreign investments and a tax system that are creating negative influences. Also, the poor performance of foreign companies in China is another factor. India is gaining ground steadily but slowly. Among the industrialized countries, the United States, Canada, and the EU are the most attractive countries or regions. A recent survey taken by the Export-Import Bank of Japan among the large 432 companies in Japan has identified the reasons why Japanese corporations are increasing or reducing their foreign investments and the relative attractiveness of various countries among them.

"Maintenance or expansion of market shares" and "development of new markets" are the main reasons for increased investments (Figure 2.2). These corporations are trying to establish a production base and sales system to meet the needs of local markets. The most common reason for investment in China was "securing inexpensive labor." The reasons for investing in "other Asian countries" and ASEAN are similar to that of China. The most common reason for investing in ASEAN is the maintenance or expansion of market shares and the second most important reason is the export opportunities to third countries. As for NIEs, similar maintenance or expansion of the market shares is the main reason for investment. The reason for investments in the United States, Canada, and EU is also the same.

Figure 2.3 analyzes problems associated with foreign investment as seen by Japanese corporations. In all countries, "lack of personnel qualified for overseas posting" is one of the most important problems. This is because highly qualified personnel who can take responsibility for starting up an overseas production base already have important roles in domestic operations and cannot be easily replaced. However, there are other reasons as well. For China, "local legislation and the tax system" create

Figure 2.2 **Reasons for Investments by Japanese Corporations**

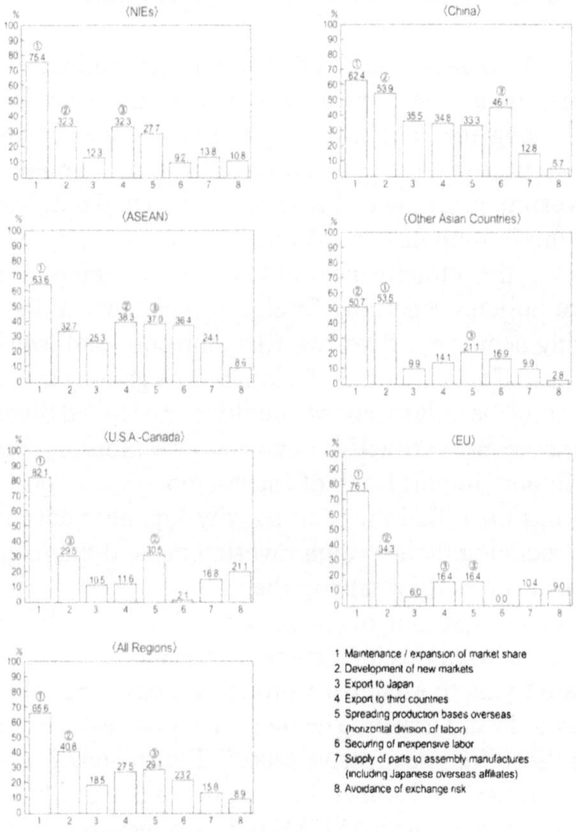

Source: Export-Import Bank of Japan

major obstacles. Lack of a proper infrastructure is also an important obstacle. For the United States, the problem comes from personnel. High labor costs and problems with the local labor forces are major issues. For Thailand and Malaysia, the local labor force is a major cause for concern, along with lack of a proper infrastructure and procurement problems of raw materials and components. For Indonesia and the Philippines, there are similar problems. For Vietnam like China, local legislation and lack of infrastructure are the major problems. For India, there are also similar problems for Japanese companies.

Figure 2.3 **Problems Associated with Investments by Japanese Corporations**

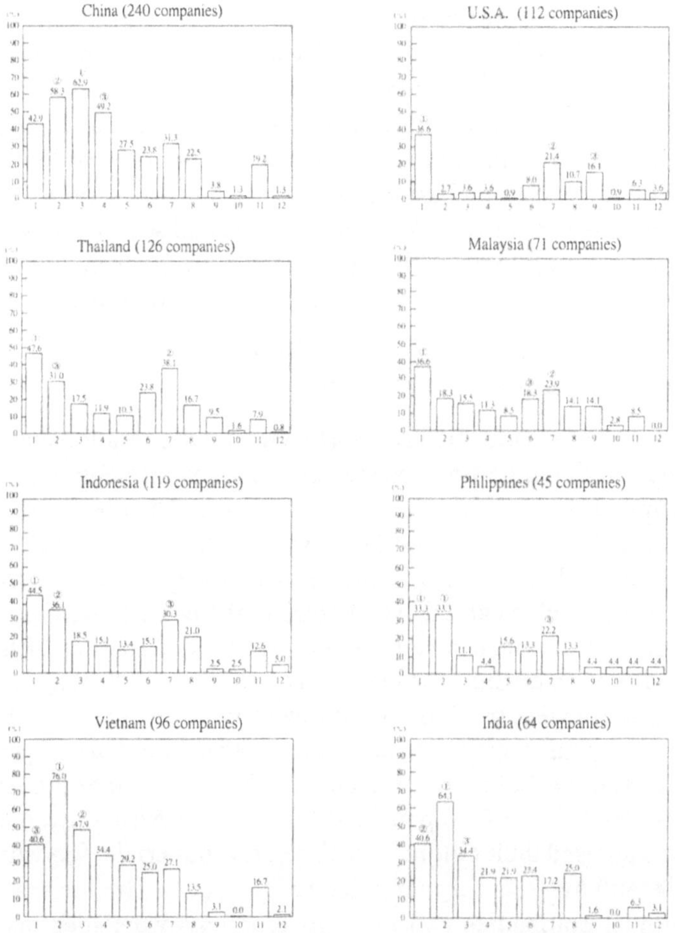

1. Lack of personnel qualified for overseas posting
2. Local infrastructure
3. Local legislation system
4. Local tax system
5. Local procedures for investment approvals etc
6. Local procurement of law materials and parts
7. Locally hired staff (management level)
8. Quality of local labor (working class)
9. Local labor cost
10. Financing in Japan
11. Local financing
12. Others

Source: Export-Import Bank of Japan

It is traditionally true that overseas production has the objective to reduce production costs, but the major objective in the future will be to establish a neutral structure against possible fluctuations in the exchange rates of the yen. The major destination of investment by Japanese manufacturers is the United States followed by the ASEAN, China, and the NIEs in that order. The most important destination for sales is the local market, which will also be denominated by local currency. In that case, the funds required will be raised in either dollars or the local currency base so that the company can avoid fluctuations in yen/dollar exchange rates. However, this calculation is now in danger because of the wild fluctuations of currencies of East Asian countries in 1997-1998. Thus, Japanese companies are now seeking more stable and secure areas such as North America and Europe, although expected profits from these operations are much lower than those from the Asian regions.

Political Economy of the Relationships Between Multinational Companies and Governments

During the colonial period, before World War II, the relationship between the multinational companies and the host governments was that between agents of the oppressor and the oppressed. The thesis put forward by Hobson (1907) and Lenin (1917) was that multinational companies seek new markets to increase their profits and enlarge their scope of investments of surplus capital. The doctrine of free trade was used to justify that aim so that host countries will accept domination of their sovereign rights in exchange for economic growth, which may never occur. State powers were used to provide security of the interests of the multinational companies, which eventually resulted in imperial conquests. The British East India Company created British empires in South Asia; the Cecil Rhodes Mining Company did the same in Africa. European governments had used their colonies to obtain raw materials, foodstuffs, and minerals, and markets for manufactured products. The interests of the multinational companies and their governments were identical in exploiting these colonized countries. However, that theory is applicable when the multinational companies are from Europe and North America and their host countries were Asian, African and some, but not all, Latin American countries. British investments in the United States, Canada, Argentina, Brazil, and Russia, using finance exploited from India, China, and the West Indies, were welcomed.

The effects of these investments on colonial economies were initially great social and economic upheavals, destruction of domestic industries, and in some cases, great famines and catastrophes. At the same times, some parts of the host countries, particularly in the coastal areas, benefited from their subscriptions to the global economy controlled by the great colonial powers.

Given that history, it was not surprising that after World War II, most developing countries considered multinational investments as instruments of neo-colonialism and have tried to develop a series of regulations to restrict their powers and intrusion in their domestic economy. However, economic interests of the growing middle class in the developing countries, particularly in East Asia and Latin America, have collusions with the international interests of the multinational companies. The result is that gradually developing countries have accepted multinational companies as a source of investments and started creating conditions hospitable for them. These tendencies have become most prominent since the mid-1980s due to two major factors. The rapid developments of the East Asian countries including China are mainly due to foreign investments. The negotiations of the GATT (General Agreement on Tariff and Trade, now called the World Trade Organization) and instructions of the IMF and the World Bank have created enormous pressures, both intellectual and economic, on the developing countries to accept capitalism and globalization and to remove obstacles for foreign investments. Individual developed countries also have created economic pressure to facilitate entry of their multinational companies. As a result, newly developing countries are competing for foreign investments and offering more and more attractive terms to multinational companies that they do not even offer to their own domestic companies.

Kudrle (1991) has suggested a number of characteristics of the multinational companies regarding their activities in the developing world. Multinational companies work as protégés as they obtain protections from the home governments. In several developing countries, Europeans and North Americans intervened militarily over many decades to assert property rights of their multinational companies. Currently, developed countries withhold economic assistance and prohibit economic aid from multinational agencies if a country does not protect the property rights of the multinationals or create entry barriers. Multinational companies also work as agents of the home countries. The U.S. government forbids U.S. companies to do business with Cuba, Libya, North Korea, and India (the restrictions are for defense-related companies and research institutes but not for all companies) and extends these rules for companies originating from foreign countries if they want to do business in the United States. Penetrations of foreign and alien cultures can have devastating effects; Thailand and Latin America show the social and moral destruction caused by foreign cultures spread by multinational business organizations (Cardoso and Faletto, 1979; Sunkel, 1972). Multinational companies in the developing countries frequently manipulate not only government decisions, but also the broader political process. Corruption, attempts to manipulate regulations on the environment, and tax evasion normally include manipulation of the political system. Recently, with the emergence of corporate sectors in a developing country, rivalry between multinational companies and the domestic corporate sector has become an important issue. The host government, in order to attract foreign investments, not only relaxes rules for the multinationals, but also multinational companies can obtain sovereign guarantees on their rate of profits, relaxed regulations on labor and management, taxation, and international transactions, which are denied to the domestic firms. Quite often, host governments, under pressure from international financial organizations, the World Bank in particular, denied government contracts to domestic firms. Recent modifications of the international patent laws, originating from the World Trade Organization, particularly prohibit domestic firms from producing independently without any collaborations with multinational companies. The problem is now acute in the pharmaceutical industry in particular. In India recently, the government under pressure from multinational companies has closed down public sector pharmaceutical firms and forced other private sector pharmaceutical companies to collaborate with the multinational companies. A number of studies for Latin American countries (Cordoso and Faletto, 1979; Evans, 1979) showed that in Brazil, Mexico, and Argentina, multinational pharmaceutical companies were successful, in collaboration with the host governments of these countries, in destroying highly sophisticated and profitable pharmaceutical industries and research organizations. These conflicts with the domestic firms will be more acute when the laws of the World Trade Organization will be implemented fully and most domestic firms in the developing countries will have to forgo their independent existence.

Multinational companies, particularly in developed countries, face conflicts with trade unions, who consider them as agents destroying the welfare state by reducing national autonomy of the host governments. In developing countries, however, where both the governments and trade unions are weak, multinational companies face difficulties only in certain countries or in certain parts of the country. It is quite normal to expect host governments to use force to destroy any opposition to multinational companies. Relaxed labor laws and environmental regulations in developing countries are some of the most important attractions for multinational companies in recent years.

Concluding Comments

Subject to a number of important qualifications, the allocative efficiency of free trade depends on the liberal rules on foreign direct investment. There are considerable uncertainties as to whether and how GATT (General Agreement on Tariffs and Trade) or WTO (World Trade Organization) rules may be applicable to many investment measures. Some regional trade treaties, most notably EFTA (European Free Trade Association) and NAFTA (North American Free Trade Agreement) contain much more comprehensive coverage of investment measures than does the WTO (or GATT) at present. There are a number of noneconomic policy concerns regarding the rights and responsibilities of foreign investors and host-country governments. Many of these issues are likely to be addressed through bilateral or regional agreements and multilateral codes of conduct and guidelines specific to the context of investments. The agreements on "TRIMs" (Trade Related Investment Measures) in the Uruguay Round final Act of GATT should by contrast be seen as advancing the more modest goal of clarifying the applications of existing GATT rules, while creating an institutional avenue for negotiation on wide-ranging disciplines on investment measures restricting trade.

3

JAPAN'S OVERSEAS INVESTMENTS

AN HISTORICAL ANALYSIS

Japanese foreign investments since 1980 have gained a very important position in the world economy. After the United States and the EU, Japan is the third leading country to decide the direction and shape of the world capital flows in recent years. In this chapter, the characteristics of Japanese investments will be examined, starting with the fundamental causes of capital outflows from Japan. In the previous chapter, the role played by the savings-investments imbalances in determining flows of capital in the world economy was examined. Here, the role of the foreign-trade sector on capital flows is analyzed.

In the current account of Japan, the surplus of trade account is far above the small amount of deficits in the invisible accounts. Thus, trade surplus provides the clue to the current account surplus. In the trade account, growth of exports was steady but imports were stagnating from 1980 to 1987 and even declined since 1990. Surplus in the trade balance was expanded until 1985. During 1987 to 1990, when imports went up, surplus in the trade balance was reduced; similarly, in recent years, Japan's trade surplus is rising due to reduced imports.

The capital flow of a country reflects the excess savings the country generates. Regarding Japan's overall balance (Figure 3.1), we can see a close relationship between the surplus in the current accounts and the long-term capital outflow. During the period 1981 to 1990, when Japan had a current account surplus, long-run capital outflows from Japan had exceeded its current account surplus. That was due to increases in the net short-term capital inflows, particularly through the banking sector (increased liabilities were more than increased assets). From 1986 to

Figure 3.1 **Japan's Long-Term Capital Flows and Current Account Balance, 1980–1998** (US$ billion)

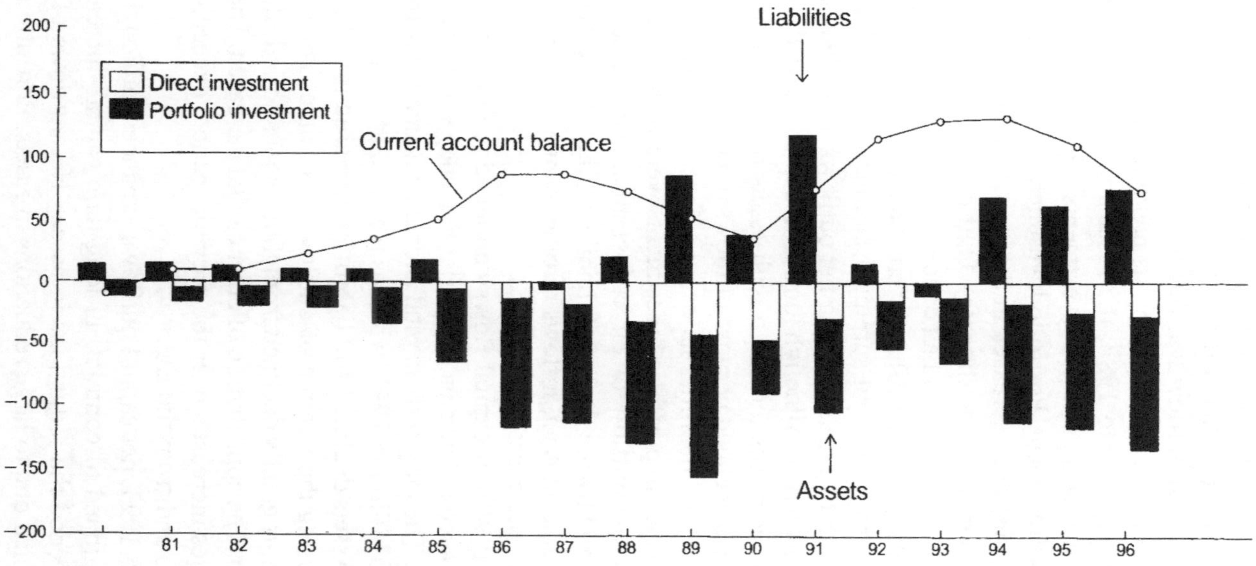

Source: Bank of Japan

1988, the short-term inflows via the banking sector were very large. In 1991, there was a net inflow of long-term capital in terms of corporate bonds and equities, although the current account was in surplus. In 1992, the capital outflow was less than the volume of the current account surplus. A large part of that outflow was due to the decreases in liabilities of the banking sector as it was repaying its previous debts.

During the period 1980 to 1987, the most important type of long-term capital outflows was portfolio investments. Flow to and from the United States was prominent. Portfolio investments were in the form of decreases in liabilities and increases in assets (when the United States was withdrawing portfolio investments). Outflows to the EU took the form of increase in assets, which had exceeded increased liabilities.

From 1987 to 1989, capital outflows were reduced in net terms, due to reductions in the current account surplus. Liabilities increased at a rate exceeding the growth of assets, causing net outflows to decline. Capital flow expanded in net terms. Although long-term capital showed a similar trend, direct investment was increased with assets rising greatly. Long-term capital outflows declined because outflows of portfolio investments declined as the increased liabilities far exceeded increased assets.

Most of the changes in portfolio investments were with the EU. With the United States, the outflow of direct investments expanded by the increase in assets and by the decline in liabilities, that is, withdrawal of U.S. assets. In Southeast Asia, inflows of other capital significantly increased along with increases in liabilities.

From 1989 to 1991, net capital flows continued to fall because of a declining current account surplus. A similar tendency was observed for long-term capital. The long-term capital account balance recorded a net inflow of U.S.$40 billion in 1991, whereas the net outflow in 1989 was U.S.$90 billion. Assets declined and liabilities increased for all types of capital flows, causing the volume of outflows to decline. The share of portfolio investments greatly declined from the previous period, although the level remained. The contribution of other capital increased. The share of the United States increased over the previous period, exceeding that of capital flows to and from the EU.

During 1991 to 1993, net capital outflows expanded, although gross capital flows continued to contract. In long-term capital, increased liabilities had exceeded the reductions in assets. Net outflows of direct investments declined due to large reductions in assets. Portfolio investments increased in contribution as liabilities greatly declined. Direct investment flows to and from the United States had some large effects on the overall developments of direct investments. The most prominent feature was a strong decline in assets. Regarding the EU, a decline in assets in portfolio investments was large but the decline in liabilities was much greater. Thus, the contributions of portfolio-investment flows were large, exceeding even the portfolio-investment flows between Japan and the United States.

Degree of Linkage

The degree of linkage is calculated as follows:

$$\text{Degree of capital outflow linkage from country } i \text{ to country } j = \frac{(\text{amount of capital outflow from } i \text{ to } j) / (\text{total amount of capital outflow from } i)}{(\text{total amount of capital inflow into } j) / (\text{total amount of global capital inflow})}$$

If the degree of capital linkage exceeds 1, the linkage of capital flow from country *i* to country *j* is above the global average for country *j*. If it is less than 1, the linkage is below the global average.

In total long-term capital flows, the degree of linkages of Japan with the United States was high and improved every year. The degree of linkages of Japan with the EU was about average. It was above average in the late 1980s, but since then it has declined. In contrast, the degree of linkage with Southeast Asia was above average in the 1990s, though it was below average in the late 1980s.

In direct investments, the degree of linkage was above average with the United States and was higher than that with total long-term capital. Also, it was increasing year by year. The degree of linkage with Southeast Asia had exceeded that with the United States in the late 1980s, but it has since declined to an average level by the 1990s. This was due to the increases in direct investment in Southeast Asia by other countries. The linkages with the EU and other areas were small (Table 3.1).

In portfolio investments, the degree of linkage was large for the EU, but it has declined to an average level in recent years. The reverse was true for the United States. The degree of linkage went on increasing. It is not significant for Southeast Asia or for other areas.

Table 3.1

Degree of Linkages of Capital Flows from Japan to Selected Countries

Types of capital outflow	Period	U.S.	EU	S.E. Asia	Other
Total long-term capital	1986–1987	1.27	1.01	—	0.79
	1988–1989	1.27	1.08	0.89	0.66
	1990–1991	1.84	0.93	1.117	0.78
	1992–1993	2.79	0.77	1.02	0.38
Direct investment	1986–1987	1.09	0.63	—	0.62
	1988–1989	1.37	0.48	1.92	0.34
	1990–1991	2.51	0.47	1.19	0.21
	1992–1993	3.73	0.40	0.98	0.24
Portfolio investment	1986–1987	1.06	1.14	—	0.57
	1988–1989	1.05	1.66	—	0.37
	1990–1991	—	1.57	0.58	0.70
	1992–1993	2.03	1.02	0.33	0.10

Source: Export-Import Bank of Japan. (—) shows that ratio was calculated.

Portfolio Investments in the United States and Europe

It is interesting to examine the role of differences in interest rates between Japan and the United States and Europe on portfolio-investments flows. The nominal interest rates were consistently higher in the United States after the 1980s. As a result, except for 1980 and 1990, real interest rates were higher in the United States compared to those in Japan. The real interest rate differentials were becoming larger until 1984, when the monetary policy in the United States became more restricted. After 1984, interest rate differentials became smaller. The portfolio investments in the United States made by Japan were fluctuating in relation to the changes in the interest rate differentials with a lag of either one or two years. In 1986, however, outflows of portfolio investments were very large, although the real interest rate differential was small. That was mainly due to the effect of financial liberalization that has caused international capital flows to grow, which in turn have reduced the real interest rate differentials.

It is important to compare the difference between real interest rates in Germany and Japan. In Germany, both the nominal interest rate and the rate of inflation were higher than those in Japan. However, differences between the inflation rates were less significant than differences between the nominal interest rates. German real interest rates were higher than those in Japan except in 1982, 1983, and 1993. The real interest rate differentials were large until 1991, but were reduced afterward. There were substantial net inflows of portfolio investment from the EU despite higher German real interest rates. Thus, the relationship between the real interest rate differentials and the flows of portfolio investments were not as clear-cut as these were in the case of the United States vis-á-vis Japan.

The spread between Japanese and foreign interest rates began to narrow in 1989. The direct and securities investments shrank because investors saw unrealized profits on their domestic equity portfolios shrivel amid a stock market slump that began in early 1990. These decreases in unrealized profits eroded their capability to withstand currency risks associated with foreign currency investments. Meanwhile, inflows of foreign capital swelled since weak prices made Japanese stocks look undervalued in comparison to foreign securities.

Japan's long-term capital outflows exceeded capital inflows again in 1992 and net outflows have been expanding year by year since then. The growth came as Japan's securities investments started surging in 1993 and direct investments edged up in 1994 and net foreign capital inflows began to decline in mid-1992. Net long-term capital outflows totaled U.S.$82 billion in 1994.

Much of the recent growth in Japanese securities has been in the bond market. Low interest rates are encouraging bond offerings by nonresident issuers. Japanese investors are stepping up purchases of these bonds for the following reasons. The Ministry of Finance eased a "lockup" rule on purchases of bonds issued by nonresident entities. (In January 1994, the Ministry of Finance lifted a rule that denies investors access to supranational and foreign bonds for the first 90 days of their issuance.) A recent turnaround in 1996 in Japanese stock prices has increased unrealized profits on stocks held by institutional investors, allowing them to cope with currency risks on overseas investments. Given this and the widening Japan-overseas interest rate gaps fueling Japanese investor's strong appetite for paper, capital outflows are likely to continue expanding through securities investments, including those denominated in foreign currencies.

Overseas securities investments and public sector loans to foreign governments have also benefited from a package announced in August 1995 by the Ministry of Finance to promote overseas investments and lending in a bid to reverse the yen's appreciation. The package was designed to spur private investors' overseas investments and lending as well as financial assistance by public institutions. It lifted a ban on foreign currency lending by insurance companies and abolished the lockup up rule on all issues from non-Japanese entities.

Japan's direct investment has been rising since the yen began accelerating upward against the dollar in early 1993, forcing manufacturers to move their production bases overseas mainly to Asia. Despite the subsequent abatement in the strength of yen, direct investment was expected to remain on an upward trend because most export-oriented companies were hurrying to restructure their businesses to withstand currency swings. Increasing long-term capital outflows was to help the dollar to gain further ground against the yen. Japanese investors, however, could become reluctant to invest long-term capital overseas if the yen regains strength again due to possible political factors or for other reasons. For the substantial outflows of long-term capital to continue, fears of the yen's advance will have to dissipate and stock prices need to rise further.

Recent Developments

Global foreign investments in 1994 were U.S.$203.2 billion, a 2.5 percent decrease from the previous year. Although annual, global, direct-investment flows decreased to U.S.$190 billion in 1992 after reaching its peak of U.S.$235.5 billion in 1990, it recovered to U.S.$208.5 billion in 1993.This recovery was expected to continue in 1994. In reality, however, global foreign investments in 1994 were only 86.3 percent of their peak in 1990.

Global direct investments fell below the levels of previous years mainly because of a sharp decline in U.S. overseas direct investments following overheated U.S. investment in Europe during the earlier years when exchange rates were especially favorable for U.S. companies. Foreign direct investments by France, the Netherlands, Switzerland, and Japan increased, whereas those of the UK and Germany leveled off. Global foreign investments that had hit the bottom in 1992 have maintained an ongoing recovery trend in 1994, though the recovery rate has slowed recently.

In 1994, the United States was the largest investment recipient as well as the largest investor. The second largest investor was the UK followed by France. The second largest recipient was China followed by France. U.S. inward investment exceeded outward investment in 1990, and the reverse occurred between 1991 and 1993. For the EU and Japan, their outward investments have exceeded inward investments, so they have maintained their position as continuous suppliers of foreign investments. Japan's investments in advanced Western markets remained at a relatively low level. Japan's share of investments in the United States has declined to 13 percent in 1994 compared with 39 percent in 1990, and in the UK, it was reduced from 12 percent in 1990 to 4 percent in 1993.

Motivations for Japanese companies for foreign investments have changed. During the 1980s, they were motivated by the yen's appreciation and coping with the trade friction resulting from the protective tariffs in Western markets. During the 1990s, they were motivated by changes in Japan's domestic industrial structure and changes in the relationships with regional economic blocks such as AFTA (Asian Free Trade Agreement) and NAFTA (North American Free Trade Agreement).

From 1990 onward, Japanese companies began to reinvest on a substantial scale using loans and internal reserves of subsidiaries in Asia, while these subsidiaries began to function as Asian headquarters in order to establish subsidiaries in countries of surrounding economic blocks.

For U.S. manufacturers in 1994, reinvestment of profits accounted for 67.6 percent of total foreign investments. For Japanese manufacturers, the percentage of total foreign investments rose from 29.2 in 1989 to 53.7 in 1993. The reinvestment level reached the 60 percent mark with respect to that in Asia.

The share of foreign manufacturing in Japan's overall manufacturing was low compared to that in the United States (about 25 percent) and in Germany (more than 30 percent). This is due to a short history of direct foreign investments for Japanese manufacturers compared to their counterparts in the United States and Germany. Since 1992, when Japan's foreign investments were very low, Japanese companies began to display their abilities to globalize their production bases (Table 3.2).

Investments in Asia

For the last few years, the share of the products produced by Japanese-affiliated subsidiaries in Asia and imported into Japan as a percentage of Japan's total imports went up. Investments in third countries by Japanese-affiliated companies in Asia were most remarkable in Hong Kong and Singapore. According to JETRO's (Japan External Trade Organizations) *Survey of Japanese Companies Abroad,* 46.8 percent of the companies in Hong Kong and 42.9 percent in Singapore have invested in

Table 3.2

Trends in Shares of Japan's Foreign Direct Investment Outflows (%)

	1990	1991	1992	1993	1994	1995
U.S.	45.9	43.3	40.5	40.9	42.2	43.8
Eurpoe	25.1	22.5	20.7	22.0	15.2	16.7
East Asia	12.2	14.1	18.1	18.1	22.7	23.2
Asian NIEs	5.9	5.3	5.6	6.7	7.0	6.3
ASEAN	5.7	7.4	9.4	6.7	9.5	8.1
China	0.6	1.4	3.1	4.7	6.2	8.8
Others	16.6	20.0	20.7	19.0	19.9	16.3

Sources: Ministry of Finance, Japan, and JETRO

neighboring countries. The reason was clear. According to the Ministry of Trade and Industry (MITI), foreign direct investments in Asian manufacturing were more profitable than those in North America or in Europe. Between 1991 and 1993, the ratios of operating profits to sales on Asian operations were at 4 to 5 percent, which were higher than those on operations in Japan itself. By contrast, investments in North America and Europe have been a license to lose or at least fail to make money, though transfer pricing may have distorted this finding (MITI's *Survey of Japan's Foreign Investment,* 1993).

As investment has been attracted toward East Asia so has trade. Sixty-one percent of the increase in Japan's exports between 1985 and 1995 went to East Asian markets. In 1985, the share of Asian developing countries in Japan's exports was only 19 percent, whereas 26 percent of its imports came from these countries. In 1995, 40 percent of Japanese exports went to these economies and 37 percent of its imports originated within them. Japan's trade with the rest of East Asia was almost as large as its trade with the United States and the EU combined.

The share of manufacturers in total Japanese imports also rose to 60 percent in 1995 from about 25 percent a decade before. More than 40 percent of Japan's manufactured imports came from East Asian economies (by the first half of 1995, 89 percent of calculators, 62 percent of color televisions, 55 percent of hair dryers, 30 percent of copying machines, and 28 percent of videocassette recorders were bought in Japan mostly from Asia). Japanese foreign direct investments were also increasingly directed not at exports outside the region but at consumption within it. Thus, it has contributed to the most striking fact about the whole East Asian area—its growing self-sufficiency with half its total trade inside the region. Japanese investment in Asia rose through the rapid growth of the Asian economies in their manufacturing industries. Japanese companies were taking advantages through mergers and acquisitions (M&A) activities. The total number of M&A ventures in which Japanese companies were involved in 1994 was 496. In 246 cases, Japanese companies acquired other Japanese companies (accounting for 49.6 percent), and in 204 cases, Japanese companies acquired overseas foreign–affiliated companies (41.1 percent). Japanese companies acquired more overseas foreign-affiliated companies than other domestic Japanese companies. The United States was the foremost location with eighty cases followed by Asia with sixty-seven cases. Asia was also second in 1993 (MITI *Survey of Japan's Foreign Investment*, 1995). Japanese companies remained eager to make inroads into Asian markets through M&A.

In 1994, the total Japanese foreign investment was $41.1 billion; out of that investment, $17.8 billion was in North America. Asia has received $9.7 billion and Europe has received $6.2 billion. In the case of Japanese manufacturers, investment in Asia was $5.18 billion compared to $4.76 billion in North America. Among Asian countries, China and Vietnam are the leading recipients of Japanese investments.

Unlike the yen's appreciation after the 1985 Plaza Accord, the recent rise of the yen until 1996 has favored ASEAN countries and China rather than Asian NIEs. For the Asian NIEs, the range of industries that has received benefits from a strong yen has narrowed because of growing competitions from the ASEAN countries and China. In the case of South Korea, for example, although heavy industries and high-tech industries have revived their fortunes, labor-intensive industries have suffered from a chronic recession and are unlikely to recover their attractiveness to foreign investors in the future, even with a strong yen. In contrast, the ASEAN countries can benefit in the future from the yen's appreciation, as the large inflows of Japanese investment to the region since the late 1980s have laid a foundation for further development. Similar to the experiences of the Asian NIEs in 1986-1987, the ASEAN countries can enjoy further inflows of investment from Japan and an acceleration of exports to Japan due to a stronger yen. Japanese companies, particularly in the electronics industry, can speed up the transfer of capital and technology to ASEAN countries.

Recent Japanese investments have a large proportion of investment in high-value-added products and processes than in the past, thanks to the improved productivity and the development of supporting industries in the host countries. A number of electronics companies, for example, have raised the local content of their products while reducing their dependency on the supply of parts and components from Japan. A virtuous cycle between the inflows of foreign direct investments and industrial development may be firmly in place. China has turned out to be the largest winner recently. Japanese companies in every major industry, from textiles to precision machinery, rank China as the most attractive place to invest. China with its large population and high growth rate promises to become an important market over the medium term.

The shift of investment to China has caused some anxiety within the ASEAN over the adverse effects this shift might have on regional economic development. To enhance their attractiveness to foreign investors, ASEAN countries are taking steps to deregulate industries and redress domestic structural problems. For example, Indonesia has since June 1993 carried out a series of measures to ease regulations governing the establishment of wholly foreign-owned enterprises and the access of these enterprises to the domestic market. Malaysia is reducing its corporate tax rates in steps, from 34 percent in 1993 to 30 percent in 1995. In 1992, the ASEAN countries decided to establish the Asian Free Trade Agreement (AFTA) within fifteen years, starting in 1993. This schedule was shortened to ten years at an ASEAN ministerial meeting held in September 1994. AFTA will cover trade in manufactured goods and processed agricultural products. By liberalizing trade in the region, AFTA should encourage a more horizontal division of labor in industrial goods by making it attractive for multinationals to build production networks across national borders.

The Asian NIEs are also taking positive steps to reverse the shift of foreign direct investments to China. South Korea, which has so far been quite cautious toward the inflow of foreign direct investments, has opted for a more aggressive approach. In November 1993, it announced liberalization measures to promote investments from abroad that brings in the latest technology.

In the mid-1960s, Japan's trade structure was at the mature NIE stage, with labor-intensive manufacturing as the leading export sector. The subsequent surge in exports of machinery, particularly automobiles, and the decline of labor-intensive industries moved Japan's trade structure into the industrialized country stage. The Asian NIEs are following Japan's footsteps in upgrading their trade structures. Trade structures of

South Korea and Taiwan were at different stages in the mid-1960s, but both are now at the mature NIE stage. Hong Kong and Singapore both were at the mature NIE stage in 1965. Subsequently, Hong Kong became a major exporter of labor-intensive manufactured goods, and Singapore pursued a development strategy based on promoting capital- and technology-intensive industries. Singapore's trade structure has now reached the industrialized country stage, but Hong Kong has lagged behind in upgrading its trade structure. The appreciation of the NIEs' currencies since 1986 has prompted the relocation of their labor-intensive industries to the ASEAN countries and helped shift their own comparative advantage to higher-value-added products. Both Taiwan and South Korea should reach the industrialized country stage within the next few years. In Hong Kong, the availability of inexpensive labor from China has helped to maintain export competitiveness, but has also delayed the transformation of the trade structure that will probably remain in the mature NIE stage at least until the year 2000.

Most ASEAN countries still have trade structures typical of developing countries. In recent years, the massive inflow of foreign direct investments from Japan and Asian NIEs has paved the way for radical change. Unlike in the past, recent direct foreign investments have been concentrated in the manufacturing sector instead of the resource sector. The ASEAN countries are seizing this chance to reduce their dependence on exports of primary commodities and are accelerating their industrialization. Thailand's trade structure is now similar to that of Taiwan in the late 1960s. Malaysia and the Philippines, but not oil-dependent Indonesia, should reach the young NIE stage by the year 2000. China's trade structure has undergone drastic changes in recent years because of the inflow of direct investments, particularly from Hong Kong and Taiwan. By 1992, production in labor-intensive manufacturing has become more important than that of primary commodities, which can qualify China as a young NIE.

The current wave of foreign direct investments from Japan to the Asian countries reduces the trade imbalances between Japan and these countries. So far, the rise in Japanese investment has been accompanied by an expansion of Japan's trade surplus with the region, reflecting sharp increases in Japanese exports of capital goods and intermediate goods. With an increasing number of Japanese manufacturers of parts and components moving their operations to Asian countries, Japanese exports to the region will be reduced, whereas imports of both final and intermediate goods from these offshore production bases will increase sharply. As a result, the bilateral trade imbalance should soon start to decline. At the same time, a more horizontal division of labor between Japan and Asia is emerging with manufactured goods making up some higher percentages of Japanese imports from the region.

In the case of Japan and the Asian NIEs, industrial restructuring will not be limited to expanding one industry at the expense of another within the manufacturing sector. Rather, it will be accompanied by a massive transfer of resources and labor from the manufacturing sector to the service sector. Hong Kong and Singapore have already developed into trading and financial centers for the Asia-Pacific region. Japanese companies will find new business opportunities in the service sector due to the changing patterns of consumer demand and progress in deregulation. The shift in the center of gravity from manufacturing to services may lead to a breakdown of the complete industrial structure (i.e., the ability to produce domestically everything that is needed), which characterizes the Japanese economy. Regional industrial restructuring allows Japan to concentrate on high-value-added products, leaving standardized and lower-end products to Asia's developing countries.

The economic crisis in Asia has dampened the prospects of Japanese investments. Both exports from Japan and imports to Japan were badly affected by the crisis. The domestic economic crisis in Japan is partly responsible for that crisis. At the same time, Japan's own economic problem has reduced the ability of Japanese companies to invest in Asia. However, Japanese companies are optimistic, as most countries affected by the crisis have revived. The Japanese government is also making a number of efforts to reduce the impacts of the crisis on the Asian economies and to solve Japan's own economic problems through expansionary fiscal policies.

Japan in Europe

Japan's investments in Europe continuously went down since 1990. In 1989, it was U.S.$14 billion, and in 1994, it was U.S.$6.23 billion. In fact, it is now less than in Asia and North America. The cumulative investment by Japan in Europe from 1951 to 1993 was U.S.$78 billion, which is about 18 percent of Japan's cumulative direct investments during the same period. Investment in the UK accounted for the highest percentage of cumulative Japanese investment in the EU (Table 3.3). It

Table 3.3

Foreign Direct Investment Inflows/Outflows for EU

	1987	1988	1989	1990	1991	1992	1993	1994
Inflow	35,375	37,447	36,695	26,116	33,125	29,558	25,180	23,767
From Japan	14	292	752	1,159	423	558	1,439	357
Outflow	14,984	21,443	30,808	41,670	25,939	23,152	28,287	25,668
From Japan	1,813	3,054	4,800	6,878	2,084	2,414	1,874	1,693

Note: Flows, excluding Intraregional investments are for 12 states. Figures exclude reinvestment of profits.
Source: JETRO

was followed by the Netherlands and Germany. The cumulative investment in the UK was U.S.$31.7 billion up to 1993. It was U.S.$18.4 in the Netherlands, and U.S.$7.3 in Germany up to 1993.

The major part of Japanese investments in Europe was in the nonmanufacturing sector accounting for 73 percent in cumulative foreign investments made by Japan, whereas the manufacturing sector's share was only 23.9 percent. In the manufacturing sector, the major fields for Japanese investments were chemicals, electronics, and electrical appliances and machinery, and general machinery.

The local purchase ratio of Japanese affiliates in manufacturing industries was higher in Europe than in any other region in the world. That was due to protectionism that persists in the EU. Whereas in Asia the local procurement ratio declined, from 53.7 percent in 1987 to 44.5 percent in 1991, in Europe it went up from 46.4 percent in 1987 to 54.3 percent in 1991. At the same time, employment in Europe in Japanese-affiliated companies went up from 127,000 in 1989 to 233,000 in 1992. At the same time, the share of Japanese-affiliated companies in total European exports to Japan went up from 3.8 percent in 1989 to 5.3 percent in 1993. The total European exports to Japan in 1989 was U.S.$678 billion. The contribution of Japanese-affiliated companies was U.S.$26 billion. In 1993, the total volume of exports from Europe to Japan was U.S.$727 billion. Japanese companies in Europe have contributed U.S.$46 billion to those exports.

It was not just a one-way affair. Foreign investment from Europe to Japan was also significant. Out of a total of 1486 foreign companies in

Japan, there were (in 1993) 468 European companies and 640 U.S. companies. EU-affiliated companies were responsible for about 5 percent of total Japanese imports in 1993, and U.S. companies were responsible for 9 percent of total Japanese imports. The technological links between Japan and Europe as a result of the two-way foreign investment are gaining importance. Both Japanese technology exports to the EU and imports from the EU are growing continuously since 1984, and in 1993, Japanese imports of technology from the EU were U.S.$118.7 billion, and the Japanese technology exports to the EU were U.S.$ 64.4 billion. In fact, Europe was the third highest destination for Japan's technology exports, after Asia and the United States.

According to JETRO's *Survey on Managerial Conditions of Japanese Affiliated Companies in Europe,* nineteen companies started new business activities in Europe in 1994, and twenty-six companies suspended production in Europe due to withdrawals. Many of the new investments are intended to rationalize and reorganize manufacturing bases. Japanese companies are making moves to invest in Eastern Europe in order to secure sources of suppliers of components and intermediate products as the strong yen demanded moving their manufacturing bases overseas. Foreign investments in Russia by Japan, for example, was about U.S.$87 million in 1994, whereas total foreign investments in Russia in that year was about U.S.$700 million.

Japan in North America

In recent years, the share of Japan's foreign investments in the United States was about 10 percent. Japan's foreign direct investments have reached their peak in 1989 and since declined until a slight recovery in 1993 and a sharp increase to $50.7 billion in 1995. The overall amount of foreign direct investments in the United States in 1994 was U.S.$504.41 billion, an increase of 8.7 percent over the previous year due mainly to the growing economy of the United States and depreciations of the dollar against other currencies.

The UK has the largest balance of direct investment in the United States (U.S.$113.5 billion), followed by Japan (U.S.$103.1 billion), the Netherlands (U.S.$70.6 billion), and Canada (U.S.$43.2 billion) (see Figure 3.2). Japan's investment position in the United States was number one in 1992 and 1993, but dropped to number two behind the UK in 1994.

Japan's direct investment in the United States (on a flow basis) was

Figure 3.2 **Japan's Direct Foreign Investments** (US$ billion)

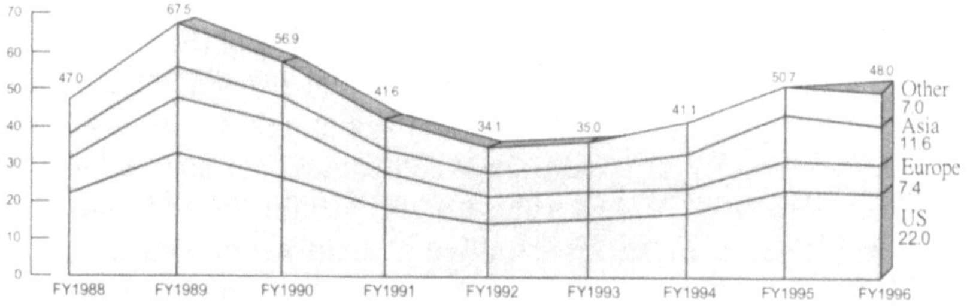

Source: Ministry of Finance, Japan

increased from a net inflow of U.S.$420 million in 1993 to a net outflow of U.S.$3.912 billion due to sharp increases in investments in manufacturing and service industries. On the other hand, U.S. direct investment in Japan (flow basis) increased by 27.2 percent to S$5.843 billion. Adjustments made due to the yen's appreciation greatly contributed to increasing investment flow, accounting for 51.3 percent of the overall flow. In 1994, the U.S. direct investments in Japan amounted to U.S.$37.027 billion. Among U.S. investment recipients, Japan ranked fourth after the UK (U.S.$102.2 billion), Canada (U.S.$72.8 billion), and Germany (U.S.$39.9 billion). Thus, the direct investment in North America is a two-way flow.

The majority of the Japanese companies (66.5 percent in 1994) make profits in their U.S. operations, particularly those in the Midwest, Northeast, Mountain, and Southeast regions, whereas those in the Mid-Pacific or Mid-Atlantic regions tend to have losses. Plants in printing, publishing, ceramics, and primary metals are profitable, whereas furniture and fixtures, pulp and paper, processed products, precision machines, and the food industry are not profitable. The reason for improved profits are increased demands, reductions in costs and increase in sales. Most Japanese companies procure their raw materials and components from local sources. The local procurement ratio in 1994 was 100 percent in printing and publishing, 81 percent in primary metals, 78 percent in textiles and textile products, and 87 percent in ceramics. A number of them (39 percent in 1994) have increased their exports to Japan and hope to increase further in the near future. In short, Japanese subsidiaries depend less and less on Japan and more and more on their host countries for supplies and finance as well.

Japan in the Middle East and Africa

Japanese direct investment in the Middle East is not significant. In 1994, there were only eighteen projects and the total investment was only U.S.$365 million. In Turkey, where a customs union with the EU is planned, Japanese-affiliated auto-parts companies have started business activities, considering Turkey as an export base for the EU. Similarly, Japan's involvement in Africa is limited to mainly South Africa.

In Africa in 1994, there were only thirty-five projects and the total investment made by Japan was only U.S.$346 million, almost all in South Africa. This is a significant decline from the position Japan had until the 1980s, when Japan had manufacturing ventures in Kenya, Nigeria, and South Africa, and mining ventures in countries with rich natural resources such as Niger, Zambia, Zaire, and Nigeria. However, a world resource glut and development obstacles in many African countries will inhibit significant future investments. Japanese business opinions identify a range of reasons for not investing more actively in the continent including political instability, difficulties in raising capital, poor quality of labor, economic instability, difficulties in collecting information, poor transportation and communications infrastructure, government inefficiencies and corruptions. Some of these arguments are valid for the Middle East as well, particularly the violent atmosphere. Thus, new major investments except in South Africa are unlikely.

Most of Japan's biggest corporations have set up industrial complexes in South Africa. Toyota has invested there since it opened its assembly plant in 1962. Almost all other Japanese automobile firms have also invested in South Africa, including Nissan, Mitsubishi, Isuzu, and Mazda. Other key Japanese investments are in tires (Bridgestone, Yokohama, and Toyo Rubber), motorcycles (Honda, Yamaha, and Suzuki), and electronics (Matsushita). Minerals and power companies from Japan are also major investors.

Japan in Latin America

Financial crises in Mexico and Argentina showed that depending too much on short-term foreign capital to fill a deficit in current balances is risky. Latin American countries are seeking to increase domestic savings and control the influx of short-term capital. They want to stabilize their macro economies by reinforcing domestic economic foundations and realize social justice by promoting social developments and improving income distribution. The flow of net capital into Latin America increased from 1990, reaching U.S.$64.1 billion in 1993. However, due to the rise of the U.S. interest rate in 1994, it was reduced to U.S.$43.3 billion in 1994. In 1994, Japan's direct investments in Latin America were U.S.$5.23 billion out of U.S.$55.14 billion, the total amount of direct investment in Latin America in 1994. Thus, Japan had a minor role there.

Japanese investment in Panama was U.S.$1.65 billion. It was U.S.$1.23 billion in Brazil and U.S.$613 million in Mexico. Of the U.S.$1.15 billion Japanese investment in the manufacturing industries, U.S.$773.25 million was invested in the transportation equipment sector and U.S.$235.55 million in the ferrous and nonferrous metal industries. Of the U.S.$4.07 billion invested by Japan in nonmanufacturing industries, U.S.$1.64 billion was invested in transportation, U.S.$1.58 billion in finance and insurance, and U.S.$511 million in general commerce.

Japanese companies have been careful about investing in Latin America. However, a survey conducted by the Japan Federation of Economic Organizations (*Keidanren*) in 1995 showed that many companies considered Latin America, after Asia, the next best fast-growing region and a promising market. The survey also reported that it was vital to promote business activities in Latin America as part of global strategies, suggesting that companies are reevaluating Latin America as an investment target.

Networking and Intraregional Trade

From comparisons of sales made by subsidiaries in three regions, Asia, Europe, and North America, we can see that the percentage of sales among the three regions in their total sales is increasing. It was increased from 5.8 per cent in 1987 to 10.0 per cent in 1993. Electrical machinery is a major item in the trilateral trade and it was exported in great quantity, particularly from Asia to America and to Europe. Europe exports mainly electrical machinery, with machinery other than electrical and chemical products to North America. North America exports mainly electrical machinery and chemical products to Asia and transports equipment and electrical machinery to Europe.

The ratios of exports to Japan to the total exports of these three regions have been increasing. The ratio of exports from Europe and North

America went up from 7.3 percent in 1986 to 10.5 percent in 1993. However, at the same time, the ratio of exports from Asia to the total exports to Japan went down from 76.1 percent in 1986 to 67.2 percent in 1993. The main imports from the local subsidiaries are paper and pulp, automobiles and foods from North America, household electrical appliances, electrical parts and apparel from Asia, and consumer electrical and electronics machinery and motorcycles from Europe. Although production bases in Asia are utilized as export bases to Western countries, the ratios of exports to Western countries by these subsidiaries to their total exports were 15.2 percent in 1986 and 16.9 percent in 1993, and the ratios of exports to Japan by these subsidiaries to their total exports was 16.2 percent in 1986 and 17.1 percent in 1993. Thus, Japan has been consistently the most important destination.

A breakdown of sales of locally incorporated enterprises in the NIEs, the ASEAN, and China in 1993 shows that their ratios of sales in local markets to their total sales were below the world average of 66.9 percent, although in the NIE and in the ASEAN these ratios were above 50 percent. In China, the ratio of exports to total sales was more than 50 percent, which confirms that China is an export base. Considering exports of locally incorporated enterprises to Japan, these three regions in Asia were above the world average, with 10.1 percent of the sales of the locally incorporated enterprises going to Japan. For China, 28.9 percent of the sales of these enterprises are going to Japan. NIEs and ASEANs exported mainly consumer electrical and electronic machinery, whereas China exported mainly apparel and electrical parts. If we consider the ratio of exports to third countries (except sales in local markets and exports to Japan) to total exports, for NIEs and ASEANs, ratios of exports to other Asian countries to their total exports were at high levels of about 10 percent with electrical machinery as the major item of export. For China, that ratio was 15.5 percent with electrical machinery as the major item.

In terms of division of labor between the subsidiaries and their Japanese parent companies, the local subsidiaries are responsible for about 25 percent of the work. This share will improve in the future and the local subsidiaries will be even more independent. In North America, the share will soon reach 60 percent, which is strongly influenced by NAFTA, which demands more local shares in the final product. In Asia, it may reach 70 percent. In the ASEANs and China, components for final products are being procured more and more from Asia than from Japan.

Regarding the division of labor for products, the share of local labor at the same technological level as in Japan is more than 50 percent in North America and Europe; in Asia, the share is now 38 percent. We expect that the share will soon reach 78 percent in Asia.

Foreign subsidiaries (i.e., locally incorporated companies) of Japanese companies are also helping their parent Japanese companies to be established in some third countries. Foreign subsidiaries are sending finance to a third country to create affiliates for the foreign subsidiaries (i.e., foreign incorporated enterprises where foreign subsidiaries have the majority shares). For example, of thirteen foreign subsidiaries' affiliates in China in 1993, ten have their parent company in Hong Kong and one in Korea. Only one has its parent, a Japanese subsidiary, in China itself. Similar characteristics are there in Singapore (with ASEAN) and in the United States (with Mexico) for Japanese subsidiaries.

Foreign Investments by Some Japanese Automobile Firms

Mitsubishi

European Operation. Production of Mitsubishi's Carisma passenger car began in 1995 in the Netherlands, a venture established by Mitsubishi Motors, the Volvo car corporation of Sweden, and the Netherlands government. The Mitsubishi Carisma compact car was developed specially for the European market.

Mitsubishi opened its Europe Parts Center in the Netherlands in 1995 to provide a faster and more efficient supply of parts and accessories for Mitsubishi brand vehicles sold in Europe. In 1996, Mitsubishi decided to concentrate production of its Canter light-duty trucks for European markets at MTE (Mitsubishi Trucks Europe-S.A, its truck producer in Portugal). Mitsubishi has made MTE its main light-duty commercial vehicle production base in Europe and has increased local content and raised production capacity to 20,000 Canter trucks a year.

Asian Operation. Proton, the manufacturer of the Malaysian national car, came into existence under the Malaysian government's industrialization policy. Mitsubishi Motors has provided Proton with all-round support since the start of the national car project in 1983, and in 1995, Proton has commissioned a new forging plant, where cylinder blocks, bearing caps, and other engine parts are produced. In 1995, MMC Sillipol Co., Ltd. (MSC) of Thailand announced the world debut of the L200

Strada pickup truck for the Thai market. Along with the growth of the Thai economy in recent years, demand for automobiles has risen to over 500,000 vehicles a year. The pickup truck is a core market segment, accounting for 60 percent of total demand, and MSC has boosted the competitiveness of its product with the introduction of near L200 Strada. Starting with the new L2000, Mitsubishi intends to concentrate pickup production at MSC and export to its global markets from Thailand. Plans call for the annual production of 50,000 pickups at MSC's Lardkabang factory for the Thai domestic market and of 60,000 at MSC's Laem Chabang factory for shipment to export markets. Starting with the new L200, Mitsubishi intends to concentrate pickup production at MSC and export the trucks to its global market from Thailand. At the Asian Transmission Corporation (ATC) in the Philippines, Mitsubishi is building a new engine and transmission plant to meet a growing demand market and to strengthen ATC's role as a transmission supply center in Mitsubishi Motor's global strategy. Construction of the new plant started at the beginning of 1996 and was finished in 1997. In February 1996, cumulative production since the start of operations in May 1994 at the Philippines Automotive Manufacturing Corporation (PAMCOR) reached 300,000 vehicles. PAMCOR currently produces and markets the Mitsubishi Pajero, steadily with the growth of the Philippines economy in recent years. In 1995, PAMCOR sold 32,000 vehicles for a 24.6 percent share of the market.

In Vietnam, Vina Star Motors Corporation (VSM) started production of the Delica minibus and Canter light-duty truck motors in April 1995. Gearing up to build the types of vehicles most needed in Vietnam, VSM started production of the Proton Wira four-door sedan in March 1996 and of the Pajero in 1996. Mitsubishi entered the Indian market when it signed a technical assistance agreement with Eicher Motors Ltd in 1982. Under that agreement, production of the Canter light-duty truck started in 1986. Learning that prospects for growth in the Indian market were good in 1995, Mitsubishi Motors entered a basic agreement with Hindustan Motors Ltd., a major Indian auto manufacturer, to produce the Mitsubishi Lancer and market it through its sales channels. Under the agreement, Mitsubishi Motors is to supply technical assistance relating to the production of a gasoline Lancer. Production started in 1997 with plans calling for an annual production volume of 30,000 units. In another venture in India, Mitsubishi Motors in 1996 signed a three-party agreement with Mahindra & Mahindra Ltd. of Bombay and the South

Africa Motor Corporation (SAMCOR), its import, production and sales affiliate in South Africa. Under the agreement, Mitsubishi will cooperate with SAMCOR in providing the Indian auto manufacturer with technical assistance relating to the manufacture of bodies for the Mitsubishi L300 light-duty commercial vehicle.

Mitsubishi Motors has provided Hyuandai Motor Company of Korea with technical assistance since 1973 and has contributed to raising the technical capabilities of the Korean manufacturer and the level of the Korean auto industry. In 1994, Hyuandai Precision, a subsidiary of Hyuandai Motor Company, signed a technical assistance agreement with Mitsubishi, and in 1995 started production of the Santams passenger model. Hyuandai Precision began marketing the Santams in 1996. Santam production uses technical assistance relating to the body, chassis, engine, and transmission of the Mitsubishi Chariot.

Together with Mitsubishi Corporation, the Malaysian Stock Investment Agency and Malaysian Commercial Banks, Mitsubishi Motors has conducted a feasibility study into cooperating in fostering the development of the Chinese auto industry through the privatization of the China North Industrial Group, the Chinese Aerospace Corporation, and Aviation Industries of China. In 1996, the Chinese Hunan provincial government approved a technical assistance agreement signed by Mitsubishi Motors and the China Changfeng Auto Factory (Yongzhou City, Hunan Province) in 1995. Under the agreement, Mitsubishi is to transfer manufacturing technology for its Pajero to the Chinese company. Changfeng Auto Factory will market the Pajero Wagon through its own sales channels under the Liebas nameplate. Production is expected to reach 30,000 units a year by 2000.

Oceania and Other Regions. In Australia, in 1996, Mitsubishi Motors of Australia Ltd. (MMAL) launched the new Magna sedan, which derives from the new Deamante. Mitsubishi plans to concentrate production of this sedan to a market other than Japan, to Australia when the Magna size class occupies a major share of the market. In 1996, plans were made for the production of 35,000 units for the Australian domestic market and 17,000 units for export. As a result, MMAL increased annual production capacity from 50,000 to 70,000 units and started to produce a V6 engine. In addition, MMAL has boosted its V6-engine cylinder block production capacity and plans to increase export of such engine parts to Japan.

In the Middle East and Africa region, Mitsubishi Motors established the MMC Gulf local affiliate in Dubai in 1995 to operate the Middle East Parts Center and supply replacements parts and accessories for Mitsubishi brand vehicles in the region. The parts center started its operation in 1996. In the first stage, it supplied the six Gulf states of Saudi Arabia, Kuwait, UAE, Bahrain, Qatar, and Oman and expanded its territory gradually. The establishment of the new parts center enhances Mitsubishi Motors supply organization in the Middle East.

Toyota: Its Activities

Toyota is the largest manufacturer of automobiles in Southeast Asia. Continued growth for Toyota in that region will depend on continuing expansion of production capacity of Toyota there. In 1998, productive capacity in East and Southeast Asia and Oceania expanded to 600,000 vehicles per year, which (in 1995) was about 450,000 units per year.

Toyota's Taiwanese affiliate Kusoai Motors Ltd began making Tireless in 1995 at its passenger car plant where it also makes Coronas. Kusoai opened a second vehicle plant in 1995 where it makes commercial vehicles for Toyota and tractors for Iiino Motors Ltd., a Toyota affiliate.

Toyota began production of commercial vehicles in 1995 at a plant in Vietnam that is manufacturing Corolla passenger cars, too. In 1996, a joint venture establishment in China was started to produce engines locally. In addition, there is another joint venture establishment with Tianjin Automobile and another local company to machine and assemble constant-velocity universal joints. That venture is also in Tianjin and it also supplies its output for installation in cars produced there by Tianjin Automobile.

In Australia, the Toyota plant near Melbourne has produced Corollas since 1994 and began making Camrys in 1995. This plant exports vehicles to Asia, the Middle East, New Zealand, and other nations of Oceania, as well as serving local demand. It has a production capacity of 100,000 vehicles a year. However, General Motors and Toyota agreed in 1996 to dissolve their production sharing in Australia and separate their operations.

Toyota serves Latin American demand through five local plants and through exports from Japan and the UK. In 1995–1996, total units sales in Latin America was 89,295 vehicles. Toyota serves this market through vehicle exports from Japan, the United States, the UK, and Australia. In addition, Toyota produce vehicles "locally" at joint-venture plants in

Turkey and Pakistan. Unit sales of Toyota in Africa totaled 43,173 vehicles. The biggest market is South Africa where an independent manufacturer has been producing Toyotas for many years. A local manufacturer in Kenya also produces Toyota under license.

Toyota's North American plants manufactured 824,000 vehicles in 1995; the annual production capacity has reached 900,000 vehicles in 1996, and 1.2 million vehicles in 1998. Exports from North America are growing, too. Vehicle shipments to Japan, Taiwan, and other nations from Toyota's North American plants increased to 66,000 units in 1995 from 47,000 in 1994. In the UK, Toyota made 88,500 Carina Els in 1995; some of these were exported to other European nations and some to 70 other nations of the world. Toyota is making a second assembly line in the UK plant to make a Carolla-class car. The new line, which has doubled the plant's aggregate capacity to 200, 000 vehicles a year, started production in 1998. It has also increased its capacity to produce engines up to 170,000 units per year. It exports engines to the joint-venture plant in Turkey and cylinder blocks and crank shafts to Japan.

According to Toyota's strategic plans, East and Southeast Asia will account for most of the growth in global demand for vehicles. Sales of new automobiles in that region besides Japan and China have increased 50 percent over the five years ending in 1996 to 3.7 million vehicles. Annual demand for automobiles in those nations is poised to reach at least 4.8 million vehicles by 2000. Toyota expects China's demand to reach about 3 million vehicles per year by that time. Thus, according to Toyota, the nations of East and Southeast Asia—not including Japan—appear to be on the verge of becoming a 7.8-million-vehicle market. Toyota is the best-selling brand in Brunei, Indonesia, the Philippines, Singapore, and Thailand. In 1996, it opened a second vehicle plant in Thailand, which raised production capacity to 240,000 vehicles per year in 1998. The Thai operation produced a million vehicles in 1996. In 1998, Toyota supplemented the product line with a passenger car developed especially for the Asian market. A second vehicle plant in the Philippines, doubled the production capacity to 60,000 vehicles per year in 1998. Plans are ready for a second plant in Indonesia. Production of commercial vehicles started in 1996 in Vietnam in a plant in Hanoi. In 1996, in China, a joint venture with Tianjin Automobile Industrial Co. Ltd. to make automotive engines was started. The venture supplies engines to a vehicle plant in Tianjin that produces passenger cars under license from Toyota officiate Daihatsu Motor Co. In 1995, a Toyota

Technical Center in Tianjin was opened to provide technical assistance to local parts manufacturer.

Honda

Overseas Activities

Honda's Motorcycle Business. Honda has two operations: motorcycles and automobiles. Of the 5.3 million motorcycles sold by Honda in 1995-1996, 4.5 million units were manufactured overseas. Honda began overseas manufacturing in Belgium in 1963 and has produced motorcycles overseas longer than any other Japanese manufacturer. Honda's motorcycle business for 1995-1996 reached 5,373,000, 11.6 percent higher compared to the previous years. This was due to the rise in sales of small-business-use motorcycles in the Asian market outside Japan, particularly Indonesia, China, and Thailand. Net sales from motorcycles advanced to ¥585.1 billion. At the same time, in Japan, motorcycle sales decreased by 3.9 percent to ¥143.6 million, a decline of 0.2 percent unit sales although Honda offered new motorcycle models and streamlined production costs to reduce the sales price.

Sales from overseas business in motorcycles went up by 9.5 percent in 1995-1996, to ¥441.4 billion; unit sales went up by 13.4 percent, to 4,725,000 units, due mainly to Asian markets outside Japan. In North America, motorcycle sales amounted to ¥65.2 million and sales totaled 121,000 units, increasing 12.8 percent and 10.0 percent, respectively. Despite mature market conditions, sales of small motorcycles were favorable. In Europe, unit sales were reduced by 25.7 percent during the same period, to 237,000 only units. In other regions, based on China and Southeast Asian countries, Honda's motorcycle business posted firm gains in both revenues and unit sales. Unit sales during 1995-1996 were 4,367,000 units, an increase of 11.8 percent. The main reason behind this motorcycle boom in Asia is that motorcycles in the United States, Europe, and Japan are used principally for leisurely rides.

In Asia outside Japan, a motorcycle is for one family, thus requiring an all-purpose vehicle. However, recently, as average incomes have grown, the number of families owning more than one unit has increased. Also, the desire of young people to own motorcycles often augments demand. To satisfy this growing demand, Honda is increasing production.

Honda Manufacturing Co. of Thailand in 1995 was the world's largest motorcycle production facility. Thailand's annual motorcycle market growth of approximately 20 percent has enabled the Thai Honda Plant to become number one. Honda's Kumamoto plant in Japan was the previous leader in motorcycle production. Honda believes that its strong brand recognition established through its motorcycle operation in Asia will also help its automobile sales in future. Honda anticipates further growth in motorcycle sales in the global market and stable expansion is expected thereafter with the development of new markets in Eastern Europe and Africa.

Honda's Automobile Business. Honda has achieved steady growth in its sales in Asian markets in 1995-1996, especially because its new plant in Thailand began producing the City, a 1300-cc new sedan tailored exclusively for the Thai market and plans to start manufacturing this model in other Asian countries. Honda's sales from the automobile business went down by 0.4 percent in 1995-1996. In North America, unit sales were down by 0.3 percent; revenues from automobiles in North America were 0.5 percent lower compared to the previous year mainly because of the decline in sales of passenger cars. In Europe, Honda's sales were down by 1.6 percent during the same period.

Honda in the Americas. In September 1995, in North America, Honda manufactured five million automobiles. During 1995-1996, Honda of America produced 564,474 automobiles at its two Ohio plants, 391,945 units at Marysville and 172,529 units at East Library. Production at Honda's Canadian manufacturing subsidiary was 110,496 units during the same period. In Canada, Honda decided to build a second production line at its plant in Alliston, Ontario. This line will manufacture a new minivan developed for the North America market powered by a new U.S.-made V-6 engine. Honda is investing C$300 million in the new production line with an annual capacity of 120,000 units, doubling its production capacity in Canada. Construction of the new line began in 1996, and production started in 1998. Eventually, Honda's overall annual capacity in North America will reach 840,000 units, with the addition of this second production line.

Honda announced in 1996 that it would accelerate its automobile strategy for the Americas, expanding its U.S. production of automobile engines and automatic transmissions, increasing U.S. R&D capabilities, and boosting local procurements in North America. Honda's expanded automobile strategy for the Americans will result in (a) a major increase in Honda's U.S. engine production to 900,000 units including two new engines, the ULEV and V-6. Almost all of Honda's North American–made vehicles used Ohio-made engines by 1998; (b) nearly all U.S. production was of Honda's automatic transmissions (650,000 units by 1998) was for vehicles made in North America; (c) Honda's investment in North America was more than $4 billion; and (d) its total employment was more than 20,000. Honda reached its original strategy of increasing automobile production capacity to 720,000 vehicles in the United States and Canada by 1997, one year earlier than planned.

In Latin America, Honda began Accord production in Mexico in November 1995, supported by its North American operations. Also, in December 1995, Honda decided to invest in an automobile manufacturing facility in Brazil for the production of a Civic model. Construction of the facility began in May 1996 with production scheduled to start in the fall of 1997. Initial annual production capacity was 15,000 units; it was doubled and total employment has approached approximately 500 employees in 1999. The automobiles produced at the plant will be sold only in Brazil, with plans to export to other Latin American markets in the future. The new plant represents a total capital investment of $100 million. The local content level at the new plant will begin at 60 percent, eventually increasing to 80 percent.

Honda in Europe. At Honda's UK plant, HUM, 29,800 units of the Euro Accord's model and 66,500 units of the Euro Civic five-door model were produced during 1995-1996. The Swindon plant in UK increased its annual output in 1997-1998 by 14.2 percent, to 110,000 units, surpassing its present full-capacity level.

Honda's stamping parts production facility at HUM began operation in May 1995, enabling Honda to consolidate business among local suppliers. In August 1995, Honda set its sights on the European market and announced plans to outsource European-made diesel engines for Civics manufactured at HUM starting in 1997.

Honda in Asia and Other Areas. Honda has been successful in advancing automobile production in the Asian markets as well. Aggregate automobile production in Asia and Oceania for 1995-1996 was 113,926 units, up 1.0 percent from the 1994-1995. In 1996-1997, Honda has boosted automobile production in the region by over 30 percent to 150,000 based on the inception of the City production in Thailand. In 1995, Honda signed an agreement with Siel, a major Indian conglomerate for the production and sale of passenger cars in India. Honda Siels Cars India Ltd. was formed and started production in 1997. The company was 6.0 percent owned by and started production in 1997. The company was 6.0 percent owned by Honda. The company has built a production plant near New Delhi for the manufacture of passenger cars. In China, Honda is focusing on automobile parts production in the joint venture, Dongfeng Honda Auto Parts Co. Ltd. Initially, all parts produced at this Guangdong plant will be exported to Honda Cars Manufacturing (Thailand) Co. Ltd. (HCMT) and incorporated into models produced in Thailand, including the City model. In 1996, Isuzu and Honda agreed to expand their product-complementary relationship in the Thai market. According to that agreement, HCMT should produce and supply an Integra SJ1-based model to be sold under the Isuzu label through Isuzu outlets in Thailand. In return Isuzu Motor Co. in Thailand should produce and supply a model, "space-call," to be sold under the Honda label through Honda outlets in Thailand.

4

JAPAN AND ASIAN ECONOMIES

Although the United States was and still is the focal point for the Japanese economy, Asia is increasingly taking the lion's share of Japanese overseas economic interests. The economic crisis in East Asia has reduced the attractiveness of that region for Japanese investors, but due to very strong links in both trade and investments, Japan is actively pursuing policies to stimulate Asian economies so as to reduce the burden of its own multinational companies.

Trade and investments have contributed to the growth of the East Asian countries that are far more than the growth rates of most countries of the world in recent years. This has stimulated demand for more liberalized trade even by Asian countries, who are traditionally developed under protective trade regimes. Now Japan's market share in East Asia is much higher than the market shares of the United States and Europe in East Asia in several strategic sectors. Japan's most important destination of export is no longer Europe but Asia. Even Japan's trade surplus with East Asia is higher than that with the United States. Ten years ago, Japan's export to the United States was three times more than with Asia; the reverse is true now (Figure 4.1).

Japan's direct investment in the rest of Asia has followed a pattern similar to that of trade, which went up from U.S.$2.3 billion in 1986 to U.S.$9.3 billion in 1994. That was about one-fifth of total Japanese overseas investment. In the early 1980s, Japan and the United States had the same level of investments in East Asia. Now the stock of Japanese investments in East Asia is roughly double of that of the United States. Japan has generated 60 percent of the world's net capital outflows in 1994-1995, so the scale of Japan's contributions in the economic growth of East Asia is enormous. This is why the recent economic crisis in East Asia is so important for Japan. We have tried

Figure 4.1 **Japan's Trade**

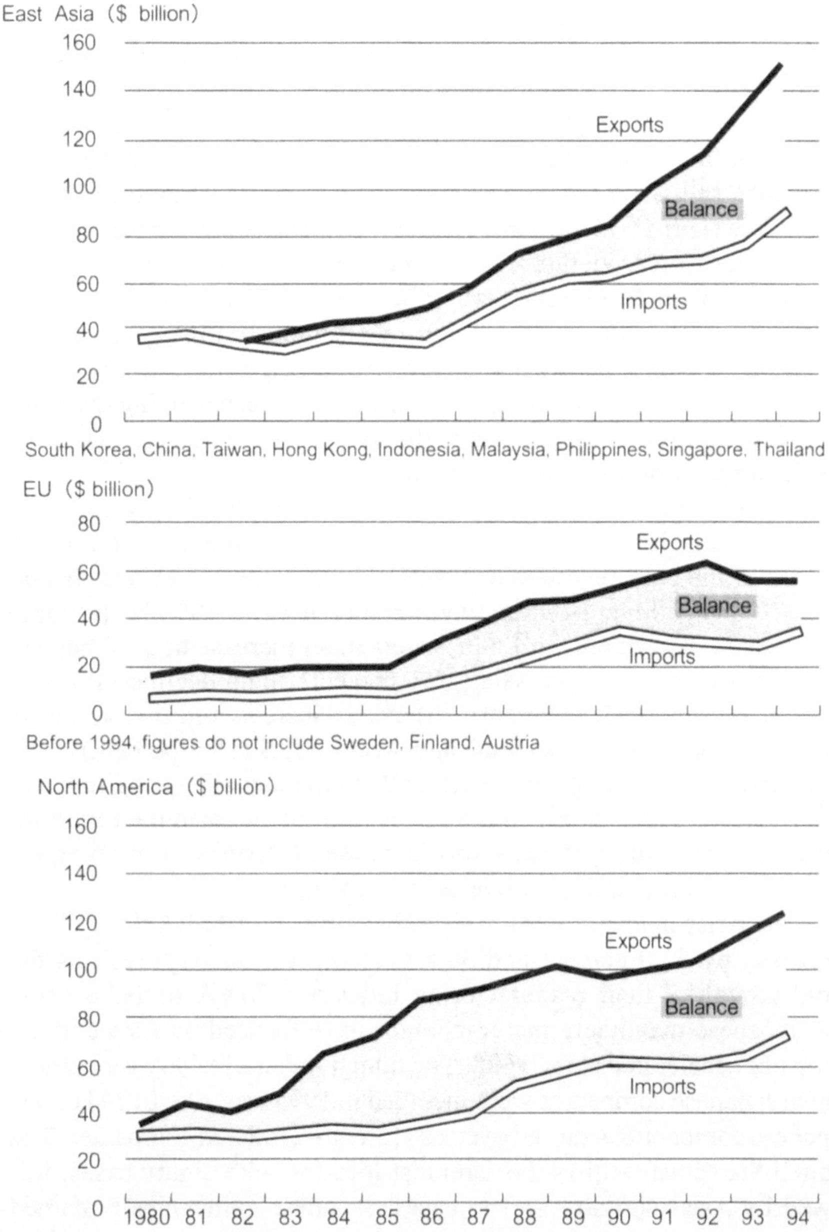

Source: Ministry of Finance, Japan

to examine the causes and consequence of that crisis in the latter part of this chapter.

Japanese foreign investment in 1994–1995 went up by 14 percent over the previous fiscal year 1993–1094, and was U.S.$41.1 trillion in total. Japanese investment in North America was U.S.$17.8 trillion, and in Asia, it was U.S.$9.7 billion in 1994–1995. In Europe, it was U.S.$6.2 billion. In the manufacturing sector, Japanese investment in Asia was U.S.$5.18 billion in the same period, surpassing the figure for North America's (U.S.$4.76 billion). However, Japanese preferences in East Asia are for China, Vietnam, and the ASEAN countries. Growth of foreign investment from Japan was about 51.7 percent in 1994–1995, whereas investments in East Asian newly industrializing economies (NIEs) are slowing, falling to 8.5 percent in Hong Kong and 4.8 percent in Taiwan, which shows that Japanese companies are expanding the scope of their operations in those parts of the world where costs are lower and goods can be produced more competitively.

Japan's foreign investments had recovered sharply. However, the absolute value in 1994–1995 was U.S.$41.1 billion, which was only 60.8 percent of the peak recorded in 1989–1990 (see Table 4.1). We characterized Japan's direct overseas investments in 1994–1995 by (a) rapid increases in investments in Latin America, an increase of 55.2 percent over the previous year, in Asia (46.1 percent) and a decline in investment in Europe (–21.5 percent); (b) steady increases in investment in the United States (17.7 percent) and Asian NIES (18.4 percent); (c) a high–percentage increase in investments in the manufacturing industry (23.8 percent over the previous year than in the nonmanufacturing industry, 9.1 percent), and (d) more Japanese companies using mergers and acquisitions (M&A) for overseas investments.

A sharp rise in investments in Asia (investments in ASEAN and China increased by 52.0 percent and 34.5 percent, respectively) reflects the rapid growth of their manufacturing industries. M&A statistics show that Japanese manufacturing companies have focused on Asia and the trend has accelerated since 1995. The total number of M&A ventures in which Japanese companies were involved in 1994 was 496. In 204 cases, Japanese companies acquired overseas foreign–affiliated companies. The United States was still in the foremost location with eighty cases, followed by Asia with sixty-seven cases. Japanese companies remained eager to make inroads into Asian markets through M&A. Asia continued to develop as a strategic manufacturing base for Japanese compa-

Table 4.1

In-House Trade Between Japanese Parent Companies and Overseas Subsidiaries

	1991	1992	1993
Export			
(a) Parent company's export	28,962	26,138	28,167
(b) Exports to overseas subsidiaries	14,487	11,695	12,291
In-house trade ratio (b/a)	50.0	48.8	43.5
Import			
(a) Parent company's imports	10,738	11,083	14,881
(b) Imports from overseas subsidiaries	3,178	3,185	5,503
In-house trade ratio (b/a)	29.6	28.7	37.0

Source: JETRO

nies. The frequent execution of M&A in Asia, which allows Japanese companies to start overseas business activities quickly, reflected the position of these companies, which were pressed to establish new manufacturing bases.

Japanese companies' motivations for overseas direct investments have undergone dramatic changes. During the 1980s, the emphasis was on coping with trade frictions and the trade adjustment due to rapid appreciation of the yen. In the 1990s, the emphasis was on coping with changing industrial structures in Japan, where production of low-technology consumer goods is no longer feasible or profitable for a high-wage economy such as Japan. Establishing relationships with regional economic blocks such as AFTA and NAFTA, in order to remove obstacles for Japanese exports, was also important. The established strategy is now to shift production to the overseas market and take the advantages of the lower costs of production and to avoid any trade frictions. As a result, Japanese companies are investing heavily in overseas subsidiaries.

Reinvestments from the retained profits of the subsidiaries form a major part of new investments. Reinvestments formed 55.4 percent of the total investments in 1992–1993 and 53.7 percent in 1993–1994 in the Japanese subsidiaries in the manufacturing sector. Asia has received the maximum amount of investments in 1993–1994 in the manufacturing sectors of the Japanese subsidiaries. The share of reinvestments among the three major recipient areas of Japanese investments is highest in Asia due to high-profit performances of Asian subsidiaries. Among the U.S. manufacturers in 1994, reinvestments of profits amounted to 67.6 percent of overall direct overseas investment. In comparison, for Japanese manufacturers the percentage rose from 29.2 percent in 1989–1990 to 53.7 percent in 1993–1994. The percentage contribution of overseas manufacturing production to Japan's overall manufacturing production was still low (only 7.4 percent in 1993–1994) compared to the United States (a little less than 25 percent) and Germany (more than 30 percent). This is because Japanese manufacturers have a relatively short history of direct overseas investments compared to U.S. and German manufacturers.

For the last decade, products produced offshore by Japanese-affiliated subsidiaries in Asia and imported into Japan (reimports) have accounted for a substantial part of rapidly increasing imports of finished products entering Japan, including copy machines, 35-mm cameras, calculators, fax machines, car radios, and so on (see Table 4.6). In 1995, 89 percent of the calculators, 62 percent of the color TVs, 55 percent of the hair dryers, 30 percent of copy machines, and 28 percent of the videocassette recorders bought in Japan were imported mainly from its subsidiaries in East Asia (Table 4.1).

Japanese-affiliated companies are also instrumental in investing in the Third World countries in Asia. Hong Kong and Singapore are the most prominent sources. According to the JETRO's *Survey on Investments in Third World Countries* made by Japanese-affiliated companies in Asia, of all Japanese–affiliated companies in Hong Kong (77 companies) and in Singapore (133 companies), 41.8 percent (36 companies) and 42.9 percent (57 companies), respectively, have reported that they had already invested in neighboring countries. Most Japanese companies in Hong Kong invested in China, whereas most Japanese companies in Singapore invested in Malaysia, Indonesia, and Thailand. Thus, geographical proximities and cultural similarities are the most important factors in Third World country's investments.

Changing Trade Structure with the Asian Countries

When overseas investments reach a certain level, shares of in-house trade between parent companies and their overseas subsidiaries tend to increase, resulting in substantial changes in the trade structure of the home country. Japan's overseas investments were just entering this stage, whereas the United States and European countries had already been in this stage for many years.

As East Asia has attracted investment, trade follows. Sixty-one percent of the increase in Japan's exports between 1989–1995 was due to East Asian markets. In 1985, the share of Asian developing countries in Japan's exports was 19 percent, and 26 percent of imports came from them. In 1995, by contrast, 40 percent of Japanese exports went to these economics, and 37 percent of its imports originated from them. Japan's trade with the rest of East Asia is now almost as large as its trade with the United States and the European Union combined. Shares of exports from Japan for East Asia went up since 1986, whereas the share of the United States has declined since its peak in 1986. China's share in Japan's exports has increased from 1990 to 1993 and it has been increasing at a very slow pace since then. The share of East Asia in Japan's imports has reached 35 percent in 1995 from 15 percent in 1970, whereas the share of the United States has declined from 30 percent in 1970 to about 23 percent in 1995.

Most important of all is the share of China and Hong Kong, which from a negligible amount in 1970 reached 12 percent in 1995. That was almost the same as the share of the ASEAN as a whole. Similarly, the share of Japan's trade surplus with the United States has declined from more than 80 percent in 1983 to about 42 percent in 1995, whereas the share of East Asia in Japan's trade surplus went up from less than 20 percent in 1985 to about 55 percent in 1995. The share of China and Hong Kong was surprisingly less than of the NIES. The net export ratio of China and Hong Kong is less than that of the NIES and the ASEAN. Whereas the net export ratio for the ASEAN is increasing, that of China and Hong Kong has declined up to 1995 mainly due to the large-scale imports of capital goods by China and Hong Kong.

Analysis of the net export ratios for various traded products shows the changes in the trade structure of Japan. For cars, there were no change between 1970 and 1993; in autoparts, the changes are not significant. Thus, in these two products, Japan still maintains its dynamic comparative advantages in relation to Asian countries. In VCRs, the net export ratio has declined from 0.97 in 1970 to 0.77 in 1993. Thus, Japan is losing its competive advantage to the NIEs. For textile and apparel, the shares have declined substantially. Thereby, Japan is losing its advantage to the Asian countries, particularly the ASEAN countries. In the case of semiconductors, Japan has gained substantially, from 0.23 in 1970 to 0.71 in 1990, but since has lost to NIEs, with a ratio of 0.60 in 1993.

If we compare the relative importance of crude oil and machine parts, crude oil imports were very important and growing both in value and in share in Japan's total imports until 1990–1991; since then, it has stabilized. On the other hand, whereas imports of machine tools was not important either in value or in share in total imports during the late 1980s, now in the late 1990s, it is highly important and much more important than crude oil in Japan's import's sector. Within East Asia, NIEs are the most important exporters of machine parts to Japan. The share of the ASEAN is much less and declining, whereas China's share, which was almost zero in the late 1980s, has obtained significant gains. China is now more important than ASEAN in its share in Japan's manufactured goods' imports. In 1995, China's share was 14 percent and was approaching the share of the NIEs. The corresponding share of the ASEAN was only 9.2 per cent.

The image of East Asia as Japan's assembly base for final products either for exports to Japan or to other advanced economies may be an overestimation. Japan is still a net exporter of color TVs to the NIEs and the ASEAN as late as 1993. Even in textiles (fibers and fabrics), Japan is a large net exporter. East Asia is becoming an increasingly important supplier of various machinery parts for plants in Japan, thus becoming very much integrated in the Japanese production network.

Performances of Japanese Subsidiaries in Asia

A recent survey conducted by MITI shows the performance of Japanese overseas versus domestic operations. Regarding net profit on sales, Asian operations are most profitable. The least profitable are the European operations. U.S. operations are similar in performances to corresponding European operations. Japanese domestic operations are more profitable than either U.S. or European operations, but less profitable than operations in Asia or in the rest of the world. Regarding labor cost (as a percentage of sales), domestic operations are worse followed by North American operations. European operations are a little better. However, the Asian operations are the best (Table 4.2).

Regarding depreciation against performance the domestic firms in Japan are worse, followed by North American operations and Asian operations. European operations are the best. Regarding research and development cost, domestic firms are spending the most and the Asian operations are spending the least, signifying their status as production bases for Japanese companies. In logistic cost, domestic firms are worse, and both Asian and European operations are best.

In North America, Japanese subsidiaries are selling mainly (about 91 percent) to the host country or within North America. In Europe, about 58 percent of the sales are going to the host country. In Asia, the situation is similar to that in Europe. However, sales are getting diversified mainly in Europe and are being diverted to Japan itself. The situation may occur in a similar fashion but at a lesser extent in North America. In Asia, where products are already going back to Japan, future changes may not be of any significance. Regarding procurements, North American subsidiaries procure about 35 percent of the requirements from Japan, but it is changing rapidly, and less and less will be procured from Japan in future. Subsidiaries in Europe procure about 41 percent of their requirements from Japan, and although in the future the survey suggests a negative tendency to procure from Japan, the significance of such changes is very low. Asian subsidiaries procure about 37 percent of their requirements from Japan and about 15 percent from other countries within the region. European subsidiaries procure about 17 percent from other countries within the region (Tables 4.3 and 4.4).

Regarding sales destinations, Japanese subsidiaries send only 11.8 percent of their total sales to Japan, whereas the American subsidiaries send about 22 percent of their total sales to the United States. Both are using their foreign bases to supply other Third World country destinations. Regarding procurements, Japanese subsidiaries obtain 39 percent from home (i.e., Japan), whereas U.S. subsidiaries obtain only about 14 percent of their requirements at home.

In order to analyze the surplus of subsidiaries networks, we define certain concepts :

Subsidiaries value added	=	total sales – total procurements
Japan's surplus from a region's subsidiaries	=	procurements from Japan – sales to Japan
Subsidiaries value added	=	Japan's exports to these subsidiaries – Japan's import from these subsidiaries.
Network surplus of a region's network with Japan	=	region's subsidiaries value added + Japan's surplus from that region

Japan's surplus and network surplus from subsidiaries are higher in North America. Both North American and European subsidiaries are generating their network surpluses from themselves, whereas Asian sub-

Table 4.2

Profit and Cost of Japanese Manufacturing Subsidiaries : 1994

	No of firms	Sales (¥10 billion)	Net profit (¥10 billion)	Net profit on sales (%)	Sales per firm (¥100 milllion)	Cost as percentage of sales: Labor	Depreciation	R&D	Logistics
Asia	3,100	1,213	40.09	4.1	39	5.1	2.7	0.2	1.2
N.America	1,304	1,350	18.6	1.9	104	11.3	3.0	0.8	1.5
Europe	921	675	6.6	1.2	73	9.1	2.3	0.9	1.2
World	5,734	3,450	76.7	2.9	60	8.3	2.8	0.5	1.4
Domestic	468,824	40,170	946.5	2.4	9	11.7	3.9	3.4	2.4

Source: MITI

Table 4.3

Regional Share of Subsidiaries' Sales Destinations and Procurement Source : 1994

	Sales Destination					Procurement Source				
	Total	To host Sales	Nonhost	Japan Regional	North America	Total	From host Procurement	Nonhost	Japan Regional	Asia
		(¥10 billion)	(%)	(%)	(%)	(%)	(¥10 billion)	(%)	(%)	(%)
Subsidiaries in										
Asia	1,213	57.0	16.2	16.6	6.6	878	44.3	15.4	37.4	59.7
North America	921	–6.7	2.2	1.3	–4.5	678	26.0	1.4	–27.6	2.9
Europe	511	–12.6	1.7	8.7	0.1	346	–4.5	4.2	–9.4	7.3

Source: MITI

Table 4.4

Sales and Procurements of Subsidiaries in Asia, Japan, and the United States, 1990

	Japan's Subsidiaries	U.S. Subsidiaries
Sales Destination		
Home	11.8	21.8
Host	59.6	50.8
Others	28.5	27.4
Procurement source		
Home	38.8	14.2
Host	48.5	85.8
Others	12.7	(combined)

Source: MITI

sidiaries can generate some surplus (about 20 percent in total) from North America and Europe. Regarding value added by subsidiaries, maximum positive changes are in North America (also in Asia). Changes in Japan's surplus are also maximum in North America. Changes in network surpluses are highest in North America with Asia a close second. Regarding network surplus, we can see that whereas both Europe (in particular) and Asia are becoming more insular (i.e., generating surpluses ever more from their own region), subsidiaries in North America are often generating surplus from Third World countries.

The share of network surplus coming from outside the region is the largest in the Asian network, inferring that Japan's network in Asia is bringing value into this region from other regions. The other networks do not bring values into their regions. Japanese firms are contributing to value creation in Asia in various ways. The network gets 22.3 percent of the network surplus from outside the region. Japan gets only 27.5 percent of the network surplus from the Asian network, the host country getting the most. Large interregional procurements of the Asian networks infer that the regional countries involved in their transactions have additional chance for getting value from providing these procured goods.

Japanese subsidiaries contribute about 20 percent in both exports and imports. The remaining 80 percent of Japan's trade is with local firms in host countries. However, for North America and Europe, the picture is quite different. Purchases made by subsidiaries from Japan and their sales to Japan contribute much more significantly toward the trade surplus of Japan.

The lesson we can draw is that the Asian network of Japanese firms is the most important multilane highway for Japan. The relationship between East Asia and Japan is maturing very fast, and East Asia, not the United States, is now the more important trading partner for Japan. The composition of trade with East Asia is changing quickly. Imports from East Asia now are not only assembled machineries but machinery parts, too. Japan's division of labor with East Asia is not a simple two-way street, with Japan supplying parts and East Asia assembling these and exporting back to Japan and the United States. It is fast becoming a complex web and multilane highway. Japanese companies are responsible for a significant part of exports of major ASEAN countries. The contributions of Japanese firms in exports was 45 percent for Thailand, 23 percent for Indonesia, 19 percent for Malaysia, and 27 percent for the Philippines in 1996. Although Japanese firms are importing as well, the net contribution made by the Japanese firms for these four major ASEAN countries are positive. Much of these exports are going back to Japan. In 1996, 39 percent of the exports of Japanese firms in four major ASEAN countries went to Japan.

The characteristic of Asian networks is that the region itself is not the most important source of development of Asian networks, especially in sales. Japan is not using Asia as much as the export base to the United States and Europe. The indigenous firms of the host countries mainly contribute exports to North America and Europe. Interregional procurement has the largest share for Asian and North American networks. Procurements of Asian networks from Japan are far less than those of the North American and European networks. The current trend in Asian networks is not host regionalization, inferring more nonhost intraregional procurements than before. Thus, Asian networks are becoming similar to European networks in terms of nonhost regionalization. Asian networks are contributing more toward the generation of intraregional value added than the other two networks. It creates value for the region and retains a significant amount within the region. Intricate webs of division of labor will make the Asian network very complex and create new additions for Japan, these will continue to help Japan's imports from East Asia, making the relationship more balanced.

Decline in export ratios does not accompany the expanding production base overseas from Japan. Many industries have experienced increased overseas production ratios. However, there were no corresponding declines in export ratios. Thus, overseas production is a net addition; there is no trade-off with domestic production.

Japan in Malaysia

Japan is playing an important role in Malaysia's development into an industrialized country. Considered here some experiences of the Japanese companies and their relationships with national development.

Japanese electronics giant Matsushita has shifted away from Japan to its factories in the Klang valley, near Kuala Lumpur. In total, about 30,000 people are employed at plants making TV sets, electrical appliances, and other products. Turnover at Matsushita's Malaysian operations amounts to nearly M$9 billion (U.S.$3.6 billion) a year, equivalent to almost 5 percent of the country's gross domestic product. Although Matsushita has the largest presence in Malaysia, scores of other Japanese companies have set up operations locally.

When Malaysia first opened up to foreign investments more than ten years ago, it had large corporations such as Sony and Sharp acting as industrial stormtroopers, setting up mostly labor-intensive assembly operations. Now, smaller Japanese companies have arrived to be vendor suppliers to the larger corporations. The work contents of large corporations also have changed. Often, Malaysia is no longer merely a link in a Japanese controlled assembly line. Now many local Japanese companies act more as autonomous units, producing their own goods and marketing them to the world or selling them back to Japan.

Japan's overall economic relationship with Malaysia has changed significantly in the past ten years. In the early 1980, nearly 90 percent of Japanese imports from Malaysia consisted of primary commodities such as wood, rubber, and tin. In 1994, primary commodities—mainly oil, gas, and wood—amounted to only 36 percent of total imports from Malaysia. The focus is now shifted to machinery and electronics and electrical products. Malaysia's exports to Japan of these goods increased by more than 40 percent each year from 1988 to 1994. Japan is Malaysia's largest trading partner, accounting for 19 percent of the country's total external trade in 1994. A great deal of this trade is due to trading between various segments of the Japanese multinationals.

Over the last decade, Japan has become the biggest investor in Malaysia. Approved Japanese investments have gone up nearly nine times since 1987. In the 1982–1987 period, Japan invested a total of

M$2.1 million in Malaysia. In the 1988–1994 period, total Japanese investments in Malaysia rose to M$17.9 billion. Although Japanese investments levels have dropped from their peak in 1990, a strong investment flow continues. Many Japanese companies have selected Malaysia as a regional production base.

Although the surge in Japanese corporate investments have brought considerable benefits to the Malaysian economy, they have also caused problems. Many Japanese companies still tend to procure their plants and machinery and intermediate manufactured goods from parent and associate companies back home. The surge in the value of yen until 1986 has added to Malaysia's import bills. Although the value of Malaysia's exports to Japan has been increasing by an average of 11 percent a year since 1988, the value of imports from Japan has gone up by nearly three times that amount. As a result, there has been a dramatic increase in Malaysia's trade deficit with Japan—from M$0.8 billion in 1988 to M$23 billion in 1994. In 1995–1996, imports from Japan accounted for 27 percent of Malaysia's gross imports. Exports to Japan only accounted for 12 percent of Malaysia's gross exports. Malaysia's current account deficit has widened considerably over recent years, reaching M$18 billion by the end of 1995. That figure caused concern to many analysts who felt that the economy was in danger of overheating. Although a deficit in the service account takes up a substantial part of the current account deficits, Malaysia's merchandise account was also now in a deficit. The government suggests purchasing more goods from the domestic economy, but they accuse Japanese companies of doing little toward that aim. Malaysia's leaders repeatedly said that the Japanese companies should show a greater willingness to transfer technology and so increase the value added of items produced in the country. According to them, the Japanese companies treat Malaysia as an offshore production base; they try to sell them old technology and they do not put local people in positions of responsibility. Also, according to the accusations, Japanese companies have created few linkages with the domestic economy. Although they might manufacture low-cost items locally, most high-cost, technology-intensive material still comes from Japan, creating trade imbalances.

Malaysia now manufactures Proton, its national car, in partnership with Mitsubishi. The Proton project had started ten years ago. Although the domestic content was more than 70 percent, Malaysia still imports many high-cost inputs, such as the transmission system, from Japan.

Proton recently signed an agreement with Citroen of France to cooperate in engine manufacturing—a move seen as a rebuff to the Japanese. Malaysia also complains that the Japanese companies should try to integrate with the local capital market, raising funds locally and listing their units on the stock exchange. On the whole, they demand more Japanese involvements in economic developments.

Japan in China

Japan's growing involvement in the Chinese economy is reflected in both trade and investment figures. A growing proportion of exports from China to Japan are produced in Japanese-invested factories. China's exports to Japan during 1995 went up by about 34 percent. China is having a trade surplus of U.S.$11 billion with Japan. The largest category of Chinese exports to Japan is textiles. In 1994, total exports were U.S.$9.9 billion, increasing by 13.3 percent on the 1993 figure. This is causing friction with domestic producers, who are demanding the imposition of stricter quotas. Other important Chinese exports include foodstuffs, raw materials, coal, oil, and manufactured goods. Imports include machinery items—steel and vehicles.

Japanese investment in China rose in 1994–1995 to U.S.$2.5 billion, an increase of 51 percent over a 1993–1994 figure. At the end of 1994, Japanese direct investments in China amounted to U.S.$8.7 billion, according to Japan's Ministry of Finance. This places Japan fourth in the table of investors in China—behind Hong Kong, Macao, Taiwan, and the United States, and ahead of Singapore, South Korea, and Britain.

Companies that are going to expand their investments in China include all the big and well-known corporations in Japan. Matsushita is investing in a factory in Guangzhou to produce three million air conditioners a year and one million compressors. MEC is investing U.S.$2.6 billion in Beijing to build an assembly line producing semiconductors. Sanyo Electronics is establishing a manufacturing facility in the Shenzen special economic zone supplying compact disc components. Japanese investments in China are also beginning to grow in Japan's global investment portfolio, although they still represent a small percentage of the total. Investments in China account for 1.9 percent of the $463 billion invested by Japanese companies abroad, compared with the 41.9 percent for the United States, 7.3 percent for the UK, and 5.2 percent for Australia. Compared with Japanese investments of U.S.$48.7 billion in

China, the United States has invested U.S.$194 billion, in China, UK has invested U.S.$33.8 billion, and Australia has U.S.$23.9 billion.

Japanese companies are looking elsewhere in Asia, as they are worried much about sudden changes in Chinese regulations. Working hours for the labor force have changed recently, quite suddenly from 48 hours per week to 40. The Chinese government is trying to persuade foreign companies to shift their new investments to the interior of China, where economic development is far behind the coastal areas. Japanese companies are concerned about the backward nature of infrastructures in China's inland regions where the road and rail systems are heavily overloaded. Moving goods from the interior through the country's congested areas is often a slow process.

Japan in Hong Kong

There are about 2,000 Japanese companies in Hong Kong. Japan is the second largest investor in Hong Kong, accounting for a cumulative U.S.$13.9 billion, and the second largest import supplier after China. In 1994, Japan was the leading supplier of Hong Kong's imported capital goods and the second-largest supplier (after China) of raw materials and consumer goods. Nevertheless, the relationship between imported Japanese goods and Japanese direct investments into Hong Kong is nowhere near as intense as it was even a decade ago. Hong Kong now obtains most subcontracting and supplies locally rather than from Japan. The trend toward localization is most marked in the field of manufacturing, which has largely migrated across the border to southern China. Although Japanese manufacturers such as Toshiba and Canon first used Shenzen, the special economic zone across the border from Hong Kong, for assembly lines, they now buy some 70 percent of parts and accessories there, too.

There is also a far greater reliance on Shenzhen factories (which are also often Japanese-founded) to produce higher-value-added goods, including laser printers, fax machines and telephones, electronic calculators, and sophisticated cameras. The cost is generally 20 to 30 percent lower than in Japan.

The construction industry is a big magnet for the yen. Few big roads, tunnels, or bridge projects are carried out without some form of Japanese participation, either in building or financing. Japanese companies have obtained the lion's share of the 155 big projects for the new airport and linking railway. Government figures show Japanese contractors have secured HK$423.4 billion worth of projects, or 25 percent of the contracts awarded so far.The figure puts Japan ahead of both Hong Kong (HK$421.45 billion) and the UK (HK$15.1 billion).

Initially, Japanese technology was vital; now, however, that local technology is as good as that in Japan and much cheaper. The preference is to go local, especially in the construction field. The lure of Japanese technology remains one of the big factors that draw Hong Kong companies seeking joint-venture partners. Technology transfers have already taken place, usually in original equipment manufacturing of electronics, personal computers, and telephones, and continued transfer of skills is very much part of government policy. JETRO itself is promoting technology transfer by sending Japanese quality control specialists to Hong Kong and China. This has been displayed by Hong Kong Telecom's deal with Japan's Nippon Telegraph and Telephone/Do Co Mo (NTT) and Itochu to push Japanese personal handy phone system (PHS) technology in Asian markets and potentially worldwide. The banks largely employ technology transfers by shipping computer systems from Japan and then relying on Japanese managers onsite and training locals in order to have a global unified setup. However, like the construction and manufacturing industries, the banking sector is increasingly turning its attention toward the local market—both in turns of technology and more client bases.

Japan in South Korea

The primary focus of Japanese investment in Korea has been on the service industry, particularly hotels, instead of manufacturing. The "Lotte" group has been by far the single largest Japanese investor in Korea, accounting for at least a quarter of the U.S.$5.2 billion that Japan has invested in its former colony since 1975, when diplomatic relations were established. Although Japan is officially regarded as the largest foreign investor in Korea during the past three decades, accounting for 39 percent of total investment, the dominance of Lotte has artificially inflated the size of the Japanese figure. Other Japanese companies have invested less in Korea since 1965 than the U.S.$4.4 billion they poured into China in 1994–1995 alone. Moreover, Lotte Hotel was built in 1970; since then, Japanese corporate interest in Korea has subsided. In 1995, Japanese investment was U.S.$296 million, U.S. investment was U.S.$513 million, and the European Union's investment was U.S.$308 billion. The United States and the EU have overtaken Japan because Japan invested earlier in Korea than the others. Japanese companies are less enthusiastic about Korea than U.S. and European companies because they had bad experiences ten or twenty years ago, according to JETRO.

Japanese companies are responding to many of the same factors that have discouraged other foreigners from investing in Korea. Korea has some of the highest wage and land costs on the Asian mainland. Its subcontracting network is considered inadequate. Some key industrial sectors have been closed to foreign competition. Protection of intellectual property rights has been a main concern. Japan faces particular obstacles because of the strong anti-Japanese sentiment in Korea. An import ban on more than 250 Japanese products imposed since the 1970s has discouraged Japanese companies from investing. Fierce labor conflicts between Japanese managers and Korean workers in the late 1980s, when trade union militancy was strong, has also damaged the reputation of Korea among Japanese investors.

The strong yen has meant that Japanese industrial companies operating in Korea have suffered shrinking profits in recent years, because the lack of a proper subcontracting network has forced them to import expensive Japanese parts. The service industry is considered a more lucrative area for investment by the Japanese than manufacturing because it avoids some of these problems. Hotels have become a main focus of Japanese investment because of the large number of Japanese tourists who visit Korea. Yet there is little incentive for Japanese manufacturers to enter Korea to win market shares because Korean companies are already heavily dependent on imported Japanese machinery and industrial components. This is a subject of worry in Korea because Korea has maintained a persistent trade deficit with Japan since 1965 due to its need to import capital goods.

Korea is now trying to woo Japanese investments, particularly in machinery and industrial parts. It has established two special investment zones near the cities of Kwangju and Chonan for Japanese companies. Incentives on offers include tax breaks, relaxed rules on financing, special labor provisions, and low-cost land. However, the program so far has failed to achieve much success. To improve bilateral economic cooperation, Korea has halved the number of banned Japanese products in 1998. They have allowed Japanese general trading houses into Korea, although their activities are limited to exporting Korean products. Industrial sectors important to Japan, such as construction, are now opened. Korean and Japanese entrepreneurs believe that the best way to promote Japanese investment in Korea may be to encourage links between individual companies rather than trying to achieve results on a broad national level.

Japan in Thailand

Japanese companies were in Thailand for three decades. They are now investing heavily and increasing their stake in the manufacturing sector of Thailand. Already, the largest foreign investors in Thailand, Japanese companies have invested U.S.$800 million in 1995, which was about half of all new foreign investments in manufacturing industries. Japanese banks are also important participants in the rapidly growing offshore lending market offering high-volume, low-margin loans.

The current phase of Japanese investment is different from the two previous phases. In the mid-1960s Japanese companies set up factories to assemble previously imported consumer durables for the Thai market, such as white goods and vehicles, using parts imported from Japan. Textile companies also set up some of Thailand's first nonagricultural export operations. The next wave of investments occurred in the mid- to late 1980s, as the yen experienced its first significant appreciation. Japanese companies rapidly increased capacity in Thailand, still mostly importing parts, but this time assembling goods for exports to Japan. Production lines also expanded into home electronics, and Japanese vehicle manufacturers, who dominate the Thai market with 90 percent of all vehicle sales, began to obtain some parts locally. High levels of capital goods imports meant that exporting to Japan and sourcing some inputs locally did not help to reduce Thailand's chronically large trade deficit with Japan, a deficit that amounts to nearly Bt200 billion annually.

The main reason for the current investment drive continues to be the strength of the yen. Moves to obtain more products locally are also spurring new Japanese investment. According to JETRO, already 40 percent of the parts used by Japanese companies in Thailand are obtained from local sources and 70 percent of these companies, the highest level among member countries of the ASEAN, say they plan to increase local sourcing.

Thailand has proven itself, despite continual political turmoil, to have a high level of policy continuity, as trade tariffs begin to fall within Southeast Asia. Japanese companies are increasingly looking to Thailand as a base to produce for the rest of Indochina and the ASEAN. Toshiba, for example, now exports refrigerators and air conditioners to Vietnam and Indonesia. Thai facilities of Toshiba are among the largest production factories in Asia and enhance cost-competitiveness in the world market as an export base. Locating facilities within the region allowed Toshiba to serve the Asian market more efficiently. After a long presence in Thailand, Japanese companies are now relatively comfortable operating in joint ventures with Thais, as is often necessary for legal and cultural reasons. Joint ventures will become increasingly important as large Japanese companies try to convince their small and medium-sized parts suppliers to set up operations in Thailand. For those small Japanese companies that are uncomfortable operating in a joint venture, the Thai government recently waived foreign ownership restrictions for new operations in certain geographic zones where the government is trying to raise the standard of living. Plenty of capital is available from most Japanese banks whom they granted offshore licenses in late 1993.

Thailand's big and profitable domestic market helps smooth out the fluctuations of the export industry. Most Japanese companies moved into basic industries such as iron, steel, and petrochemicals that will provide backward linkages for several industries.

There are two important problems: Labor costs are rising without corresponding gains in productivity levels; the massive amounts of red tapes show few signs of dissipating. Finding skilled labor and people qualified to staff middle management positions is very difficult in Thailand; there are problems of languages, too. Japan also finds the Thai tendency to change jobs frequently quite alien. In the early days of Japanese investment, the lack of skilled workers was not a problem. Wages for unskilled Thais were low and the country basically was seen as a place to do assembly. Still, wages for unskilled workers are also rising. Japanese companies report that wages for both skilled and unskilled workers in Thailand are now the highest in the ASEAN excepting Singapore. From the Japanese business perspective, Thailand risks pricing itself out of the assembly market without being able to make a complete leap into more value-added industries and services. According to Japanese companies, significant changes in Thailand's alien business law and customs procedures are also necessary. Limits on having just five expatriate employees per division and the costs involved in complying with labor and customs law are cited by JETRO as the number one complaint of Japanese companies operating in Thailand.

Case Study: SONY in Asia

SONY, the Japanese consumer electronics group involved in a U.S.$29 million joint venture in China is typical of the new wave of Japanese investments. It is part of a tidal wave of money breaking over many of Japan's Asian neighbors, but increasingly focused on China. The potential political and financial risks of investing in China are huge, but SONY like others can no longer afford to be hypercautious about entering a market of more than 1 billion people whose demand for consumer electronics is growing at roughly 20 percent a year.

SONY's experiences in East Asia illustrate the Japanese investment trend in the region. First, ever-larger investments have followed cautious steps into the local assembly of largely imported components for the local market and for exports to other Asian countries, the United States, and increasingly to Japan. For SONY's investments in the region, the main driving force has been the fast growth of East Asian markets, now expanding at 15 to 20 percent a year, the fastest growing region in the world. Over the past decades, SONY's sales in the region have grown from 6 to 20 percent of the group total.

SONY first set foot in East Asia in 1967, when the acquisition of another Japanese company happened to include a radio and telephone producing unit in Taiwan. Its second step into the region, a television tuner factory in South Korea, also came as the result of an acquisition in 1973. Then came a nine-year gap, during which SONY made no East Asian investments, focusing instead on its home ground. Then the Japanese domestic market was experiencing the kind of growth only now seen among Asian high flyers. A Malaysian radio, walkman, and telephone plant opened in 1984 followed by a videocassette recorder factory in Taiwan in the same year. However, after the 1985 Plaza accord, the worlds' leading economies agreed to cooperate to devalue an overvalued dollar. That was the turning point for the yen, which touched ¥263 to the dollar that year and has since moved to around ¥100, in the process rendering large swathes of Japanese domestic manufacturing uncompetitive. SONY took the only option: to move production offshore in search of cheaper costs and easier exchange rates. By the end of that decade, eight more SONY plants were in operation in Singapore, Malaysia, and Thailand; since then, they have been joined by five more—in Indonesia, Singapore, China, Vietnam, and India. Now, 25,000 of SONY's 138,000 employees are in Asia, within which Malaysia has the highest number of staff—185,000—of any single country outside Japan. Local content is high, up to 97 percent for video recorders and televisions in Malaysia. This includes most components made in other Asian countries, an illustration of how Japanese investment has contributed to the growing interdependence of Asian economies. SONY's Malaysian color televisions contain picture tubes made at other plants in Asia.

The Plaza accord and the need to compensate for the high yen has influenced SONY's decision to expand in Asia; however, there are other reasons. Making investment in Asia would raise purchasing power in Asian countries so that they would become more important markets for Asian products. In Malaysia, Japanese companies alone account for 6 percent of the gross domestic product. Another factor behind Asian expansions was the desirability of avoiding high import duties on assembled goods. Local assembly of imported parts was the obvious answer, as SONY and many other Japanese companies also discovered in Europe. Yet, as in Europe, that pressure has now started to recede as more industrialized Asian countries begin to reduce their tariff barriers. The Philippines, Malaysia, and Indonesia have all promised to reduce import duties faster and farther than the minimum required in WTO recommendations. The company philosophy of keeping its share of the regional sales roughly equal to the share of that region in the world consumer electrical market has guided SONY. Thus, Asia's one-fifth share of SONY's sales compares with a quarter in Europe and a quarter in North America. However, Asian economics dynamism is such that this share may soon go up to 40 to 50 percent of SONY's world sales. SONY's share in North America and Europe will remain be very high, however, as SONY does not want to lose its share in mature markets.

Case Study: NTT in Asia

Telecommunication giant Nippon Telegraph and Telephone Corp. is cautiously but steadily gearing up to go globally and it is using Asia as a steppingstone. Currently, there are three major alliances in the world telecommunications sector; concertedly headed by BT and MCI Communications Corp., the second largest carrier in the United States; Global One led by Deutsche Telekom, France Telekom, and the U.S.-based Sprint Corp.; and World Partners, which includes AT&T, KDD, and Singapore Telecommunications Ltd.

Japan's international telecommunications market is worth only about ¥500 billion, compared with the domestic market's value of ¥10 trillion. The importance of launching the international service will increase as demand grows for multimedia and with intensified worldwide competition. The fast-growing Asian economy will not only mean that telephone networks will expand further, with more multinational companies establishing their business footholds in Asia, the demand for highly advanced multimedia services will also grow in the coming years.

NTT has been investing in Asia since the government allowed it to participate in phone service projects in 1992. Since then, it has invested in Thailand, the Philippines, Indonesia, India, and Vietnam to help build local telephone networks and it has been helping China to develop and design its various network systems.

The company is also a major participant in a multimedia project to build a "cybercity" in Malaysia called the "multimedia super corridor," and it has applied for a telecommunications license in Singapore jointly with BT.

NTT has established the Asian Multimedia Forum (AMF) in Singapore with participation from seventeen telecommunications organizations from eight Asian nations; this will cooperate to develop appropriate services and technology to meet the region's demand for multimedia and to promote mutual participation in various multimedia projects in Asia. Through AMF, NTT is trying to spread a certain standard based on NTT technology throughout Asia. More than half of non-Japanese AMF members are companies that NTT has either invested or with which it has established a joint venture.

Given the growing importance of the communication systems in the world economy, NTT provides the technology and expertise to the Asian countries to participate fully in the Information Age.

The Role of Yen as the "International Currency" in Asia

One of the most important features of Japan's close link with the rest of Asia is the usage of the Japanese yen in international transactions. This change has encouraged the emergence of the "Yen Area" in Asia, similar to the "D-Mark bloc" in Europe. The Japanese government for many years was opposed to such ideas, because as a reserve currency of international payments the yen then would create restrictions on applications of monetary policies by the domestic monetary authority, that is, it will restrict the Bank of Japan's role. Recently, however, there is growing opinion that the benefits may outweigh the costs of the yen as an international reserve currency in the "Yen area." Asian governments are also showing increasing interest in the wider use of the yen.

Internationalization of the yen has several advantages for Japan. Japanese companies want to receive benefits from international trade. When most trade is denominated in U.S. dollars, the costs to Japan's exporters of a higher yen are immediate and damaging. If foreign companies accept yen invoices, damage caused by the appreciation of the value of the yen can be restricted. That was the main cause of internationalization of yen in recent years. In 1970, less than 1 percent of Japan's exports were denominated in yen. By 1986, the figure had risen to 36.5 percent. Since then, progress has been slower; by 1995, the figure had risen to just 38 percent. For imports, the yen denomination is up from less than 10 percent of total imports in 1986 to more than 24 percent in 1995. The proportion of total Japanese exports to Asia denominated in the yen rose from 39 percent in 1986 to 48 percent in 1995. Imports went up from 9.2 to 34 percent.

The increasing use of the yen in the capital markets has benefits, too. Between 1985 and 1995, Japan's financial institutions had experienced a capital loss on their holdings of foreign currency assets of ¥37,000 billion. If they had held more of those assets in yen, the losses for Japan's banks and life insurance companies would have been much less, as they probably could have avoided losses due to the increasing value of the yen. Japan's recent currency account deficit (U.S.$ 130 billion in 1994–1995) encourages capital outflows into overseas assets, but institutions are anxious to shift a large part of that into yen assets. In the past few years, Japanese investors have begun increasing their holdings of yen-denominated assets. They would like that process to continue, and there are signs that it is spreading to Asian bond markets. The Japanese government can ask the U.S. government to issue yen bonds, but there is little possibility of that. So they are trying to encourage Asian countries to issue more yen assets. Asian countries, if they borrow in yen, do not have to pay increasing amounts if the yen appreciates against U.S. dollars, as it had happened during the 1990s. Their savings on debt repayments will be enormous. Also, the yen's rise against the U.S. dollar can make their goods cheaper in Japan and thus would increase their exports to Japan.

Over the last decades, the Asian currencies were tied to the U.S. dollar; appreciations of the yen against the U.S. dollar also have depreciated the Asian currencies, thus fueling domestic inflation in other Asian countries. However, there is a cost. Japan's own currency-induced problems (as an appreciating yen makes Japanese export goods ever more expensive abroad) have resulted in substantial Japanese investments in Asia; that process will be slowed if the yen replaces the U.S. dollar in intraregional trade. One of the factors contributing to the recent economic crisis in Asia was the excessive dependence of Asian economies on the U.S. dollar, which has reduced the competitiveness of these countries by overvaluating their exchange rates. Now, Asian countries are gradually moving away from the U.S. dollar, partly due to the emergence of the euro as an alternative. Given the importance of Japan in the regional economy of East Asia, increasing use of the yen will stabilize export earnings and the macroeconomic performances of these countries.

However, various Asian countries take the potential gains in the Asian yen-denominated debt sector more seriously than anything else. The yen's rise in recent years raised the real value of their national debt. The proportion of East Asian countries debt denominated in yen rose from 17.9 percent of the total debt in 1980 to 30 percent in 1993. As the Japanese currency has appreciated, debt-service costs have risen sharply. The solution is for countries to shift their currencies toward the yen. In 1995, the central banks of Malaysia and Thailand raised their holdings of yen as a proportion of their total reserve. Other countries are expected to follow suit. These pressures have raised the importance of the yen in Asian financial markets. Weighting given to the yen in currency baskets has increased for most Asian currencies. Taiwan has increased the yen's weighting from 6 percent of the currency's total in the early 1990s to more than 30 percent in 1995. This process has been reflected in the gradual strengthening of the relationship between the yen and Asian currencies. A defacto yen currency area is already slowly merging.

However, there are problems due to the nature of Japan's capital market, which is highly regulated. As a result, international investors are not attracted in holding yen. Compared to the U.S. market, there is a marked shortage of Treasury Bonds and Financing Bills in the Japanese market; consequently, the market lacks adequate depth. Adequate liquidity is not necessarily available to match all the diverse forms of demands. The markets are hampered from efficiently establishing a yield curve that can serve as an indicator for financial markets. That restricts access to risk-hedging measures. Withholding taxes on the interest earnings received by nonresidents may be one of the obstacles to nonresident participation in Japan's government bond markets.

However, due to the importance of the Japanese economy in Asian regions and the diminishing attraction of the U.S. dollar (in spite of recent improvements), something like a yen area may emerge within the next decade. Asian countries are experiencing a serious credit crunch in trade finance as a consequence of the economic difficulties that have followed the currency crisis. Although trade finance has been supplied mainly in dollars, it is desirable for Japan to respond to this credit crunch by expanding the available facilities for yen financing in the near future.

The Role of Japan in Regional Developments

There are complaints about Japan's role in Southeast Asia. The major complaint is that Japan has been reluctant to share its technology. Japan has done little to mitigate the effect of the rise of the yen on Malaysia and other developing countries still heavily dependent on Japanese imports. They also feel that Japan has failed to open its markets while expecting access to market in the developing world. Japan has also shown little interest on the formation of an East Asian Economic Caucus (EAEC), a body first proposed by Malaysia in 1991. According to Malaysia, when the world is divided into competing trade blocks, the fast-growing countries in East Asia should join to discuss common positions on trade. Yet Japan is more concerned with its relations with the United States than with Malaysia and other countries in Southeast Asia and the United States is not in favor of the EAEC. Japan is sensitive to fears expressed in some Asian countries of growing Japanese economic dominance that conjures up memories of Japan's "greater co-prosperity sphere." For these reasons, Japan is unlikely to take a lead role in Asia.

Japan is involved seriously in other regional groupings, however. It is a leading participant in the Asia Pacific Economic Cooperation Forum (APEC) and the ASEAN Regional Forum, a recently formed regional body on security issues. A deepening integration among the region's previously disparate economies has accompanied Japan's turn toward Asia. There is growing interdependence, not just between Japan and Asia, but also for the first time in their histories among Asian economies themselves. Asian economies sales to each other—including Japan—increased from 30 percent of their total exports to nearly 45 percent during the decade up to 1995. Their exports to the United States declined from just less than 35 percent to 25 percent over the same period. A mixture of factors is at work in driving Japan's economic assault on its neighbors. East Asian demands for consumer goods and industrial plants, political and economic constraints on growth in Japanese exports to the United States, and the fresh pressure on Japanese industry brought by the rise in the yen have motivated Japanese companies to seek cheaper production abroad.

Japan's economic march into Asia comes at a time when the political balance of the region is also changing. Japan is still adjusting to the end of the Cold War, which has diminished the need for a military alliance with the United States. This change has paved the way for a new generation of politicians to reappraise "Japan-United States" links in a more neutral light.

So far, trade with APEC has grown fast enough to defuse serious resentment of Japan's preeminence except the occasional grumble from South Korea. However, Japan does admit that its trade surplus plus the demands of the rice farmers make it reluctant to push ahead with APEC's vision of free trade. Moreover, Japan remains divided on the role of APEC. MITI has been an enthusiastic supporter. The foreign ministry, however, was initially reluctant to back anything that might cut across a more local regional body—ASEAN—which is strongly supported by the ministry. The foreign ministry continues to emphasize that APEC should be merely consultative—ASEAN style—whereas MITI officials lean the other way, toward free-trade rules.

The Japanese government could not ignore the "crisis" in East Asia. It has recently taken a series of measures to solve its own economic problem and to help the countries in East Asia. The package of the financial and trade support to East Asia in 1998 has reached US$30 billion of which U.S.$15 billion was available for medium- to longer-term financial need. Another U.S.$15 billion was available for short-term needs to provide adequate liquidity to these affected countries. We have to remember that the total support of the IMF was about U.S.$13 billion. In addition, Japan's Export-Import Bank would provide guarantees on international bank loans, sovereign bonds, and export credits to East Asian countries. Japan also has established an "Asian Currency Crisis Support Facility" that will provide interest subsidies to allow borrowers to raise funds at a smaller cost. In 1996, before the crisis had emerged, Japan had suggested the establishment of an Asian Monetary Fund separate from the control of the International Monetary Fund. However, due to the objections raised by the U.S. government, it did not materialize. The IMF has responded to the Asian crisis by contracting credit further through restricted monetary and fiscal policies while these countries were suffering from a liquidity crisis due to the fall of their export revenues and outflows of foreign capital.

Total Japanese bank lending to East Asia in 1998 was about U.S.$274 billion. Thus, the solution of the Japanese banking crisis cannot only stimulate Japanese economy, but also provides increasing liquidity to the crisis-affected countries. The Japanese government has started nationalizing banks in Japan that are on the verge of bankruptcy and providing public funds to all banks that need it so as to protect them from collapsing. These, along with fiscal expansions and reductions of personal and corporate tax rates, will stimulate the economy by providing an adequate capital base to the banks, which in turn will help them to provide new investment funds for the corporate sector. Any upturn of the Japanese economy will have significant positive impacts on the economy of East Asia.

East Asian countries have taken a number of measures as part of their economic restructuring program supported by the IMF. The outcome is uncertain, particularly because of the political disturbances in Indonesia and Malaysia. Certainly, the structure of the East Asian economy will change. Taking advantage of the economic crisis, foreign companies, mainly from the United States, UK, Germany, Singapore, and Taiwan, are taking over a number of companies in East Asia through mergers and acquisitions; Japan is playing a minor role. In the future, Japanese companies may not play such a vital role in East Asia as they do now.

5

IMPACTS OF OVERSEAS BUSINESS ACTIVITIES ON TRADE AND DOMESTIC PRODUCTION IN JAPAN

In recent years, the Japanese trade structure has been changing considerably with the increased imports of manufactured products and increased exports of capital goods. Trade with subsidiaries through direct investment are considered the most important factor of this change in the trade structure. There are three main effects we need to consider: (a) the export substitution effect by which Japanese exports decrease by being substituted by local production made by subsidiaries; (b) the export inducement effect by which Japanese exports increase because of the increased demands for capital and intermediate goods coming from subsidiaries; (c) the import enhancement effect by which Japanese imports increase because subsidiaries export their products back to Japan. It was estimated that in terms of the export inducement effect, the ratio of capital goods exported for the subsidiaries to the total capital goods exports was 36.6 percent in 1993. In terms of the import inducement effect, the ratio of consumers goods imported from subsidiaries to the total imports of consumers goods were 19.2 percent in 1993. The overall picture on the trade balance was positive, that is, the subsidiaries have created net export effects. There are a number of reasons for that. Exports of capital goods will increase considerably at the early stage of investments, as it will take a long time for foreign subsidiaries to produce the machineries locally.

The distortions caused by foreign investments on domestic production, however, are significant. Investments in plant and machinery made by Japan in foreign ventures were a large part of the total domestic activity. In 1993, it was 17.5 percent of domestic manufacturing investments. Although it is difficult to say that foreign investments have replaced domestic investments because of movements of the exchange rate of the yen, they certainly were an important part of the intended private domestic investments. Regarding employment, the net impact of the textile sector in 1993 was still positive, but it is expected to create large-scale unemployment particularly due to the effects of imports from China and other Asian countries. In the case of electrical machinery, the impact is already negative and it will decrease further. In the case of transport equipment, the impact in 1993 was highly positive, but the positive impact is declining. In the case of other machinery, the impact is still positive and it is expected to last.

It is important to examine the impacts of Japanese foreign investments on the Japanese economy. It is possible to obtain these from the survey on Japanese multinational companies conducted by the MITI. The following analysis is based on the latest MITI survey conducted in 1996. The method of analysis is presented in the appendix at the end of the chapter.

Impacts on Trade

In recent years, the Japanese trade structure has been changing considering the increase of imports of manufactured products such as consumer goods and the increase of exports of capital goods. Trade with locally incorporated enterprises through direct investments is considered to be the important factor of this change in the trade structure.

Overseas Business Activities

The following are possible impacts that overseas business activities may have on export and imports.

Export Substitution Effect. Japanese exports will decline because of substitutions of Japanese exports by the products of the foreign operations of Japanese multinationals.

Export Inducement Effect. Japanese export will increase due to the increased export of Japanese machinery for Japanese foreign subsidiaries.

Import Inducement Effects. Imports from foreign subsidiaries will go up, so Japanese imports will go up.

In terms of the export inducements effect, the ratio of capital goods exported to Japanese subsidiaries to the total capital goods exports was 36.6 percent in FY 1993. At the same time, consumer goods imports from Japanese subsidiaries to the total imports of consumer goods was 19.2 percent. Thus, we can see, overseas business activities can have a great impact on the future trade structure of Japan. (See Figures 5.1 and 5.2.)

Figure 5.1 **Ratio of Consumer Goods Exports to the Locally Incorporated Enterprises to Japan's Total Consumer Goods Exports**

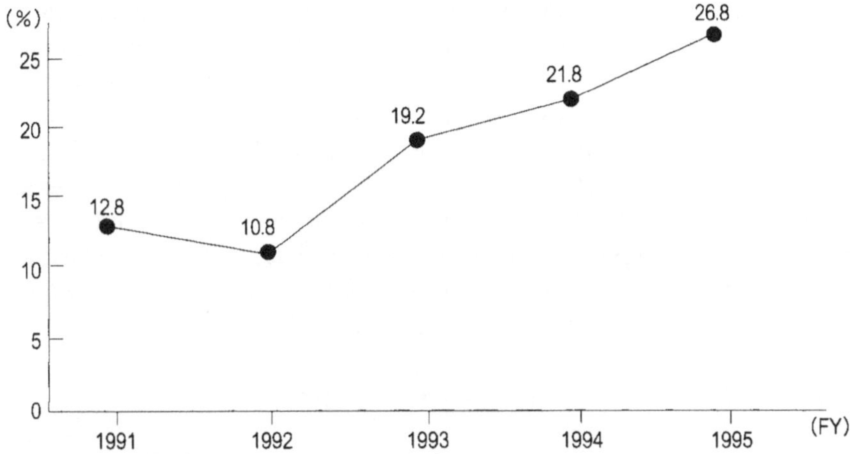

Source: JETRO

Figure 5.2 **Ratio of Capital Goods Exports to Locally Incorporated Enterprises to Japan's Total Capital Goods Exports**

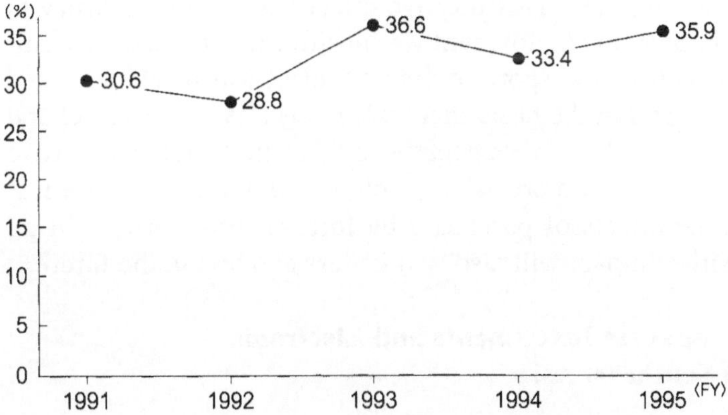

Source: JETRO

Impacts on Trade Balance of Overseas Business Activities

The analysis of recent trade structure shows that the export inducement effect of foreign subsidiaries are more prominent than the export substitution effect or the import effect, and on the whole, Japanese subsidiaries are contributing positively on the balance of trade. Exports of equipment for production are expected to increase at the early stages of the establishment of subsidiaries. At the same time, it takes a long time to increase local content unless the host country is technologically developed. Overseas activities had a positive impact in FY 1993, but they were expected to have a reduced positive impact from FY 1994 onward because of rapid technology transfers to foreign subsidiaries (see Figure 5.3).

Impacts on Domestic Production and Employment

Investments and reinvestments made by Japanese subsidiaries (and affiliates) are equivalent to 17.5 percent of the Japanese domestic investments in FY 1993 (see Figure 5.4). Due to the distortion caused by a strong yen and price differences between Japan and abroad, these foreign investments were possibly made instead of investments at home. Thus, they might have considerable negative impact on domestic production and employment. However, as we have seen, foreign investments also increase demands for exports of investment goods to foreign subsidiaries and affiliates. This positive effect varies from industry to industry. The impact on employment was positive in processing/assembly industries such as transport equipment, electrical machinery, and other machinery, and in the basic materials industries such as steel and chemicals. However, there were negative effects on the labor-intensive sectors such as textiles and precision machinery in FY 1993. Since it is expected that the effects of purchases by foreign subsidiaries will go down, the positive impact will also will be less and less in the future.

Case Study: Japanese Investments and Electronic Industries in Southeast Asia

Southeast Asian countries have started their export-oriented consumer-goods industries during the early 1960s with the help of Japan and Western European multinational companies. By the early 1970s, U.S. multinationals have started assembling semiconductors in the ASEAN re-

Figure 5.3 **Impacts of Overseas Business Activities on Trade Balance** (¥trillion)

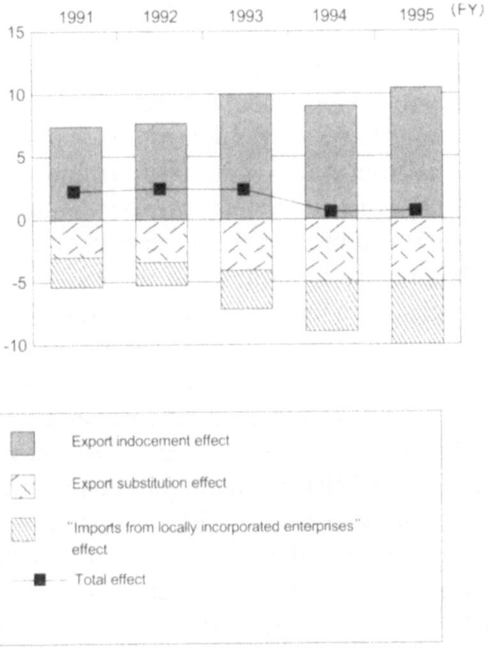

Source: JETRO

Figure 5.4 **Impacts of Overseas Business Activities on Domestic Employment in Major Industries** (number of employees)

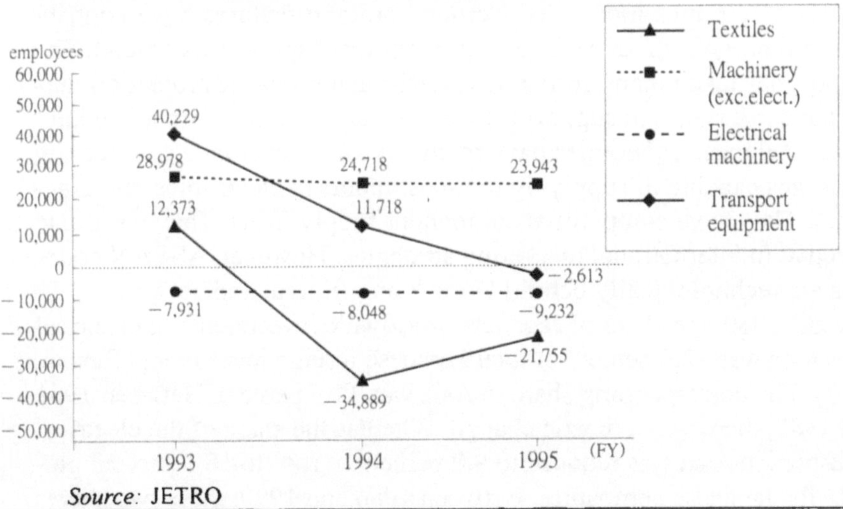

Source: JETRO

gion. This section will analyze the characteristics of this development and the role of the Japanese multinationals on the economy of Japan and that of host countries.

ASEAN countries have encouraged foreign investments in many ways. Governments have waived local-content requirements for foreign firms, whereas these rules were applied for domestic manufacturers. The firms were also allowed to import raw materials, semiprocessed goods, and capital equipment free of tariffs. Import/export regulations have been streamlined for export ventures. In the semiconductor industry, linkages with local manufacturers were modest. The processes, mainly assembly lines that multinational companies transferred to ASEAN-based subsidiaries, are highly labor-intensive. Since the early 1980s, automating the semiconductor assembly plants in the region has gained momentum. It is possible, due to automation that multinational companies can no longer save labor costs from offshore operations. Thus, they may phase out their investments and establish highly automated facilities in the major market area. So the policy makers in ASEAN countries are increasingly concerned about the future of the semiconductor industry.

Singapore has already made major change in its electronics industries. It is trying to diversify its electronics industries from semiconductors to consumer and industrial electronics. Singapore's electronics industries are highly competitive but not autonomous, and those in Hong Kong have remained at a comparatively low level of technology. Korea and Taiwan have developed both autonomous and internationally competitive electronics industries. Certain common features have contributed to their growth. In each case, government support was crucial. The support has taken many forms, from tariff and nontariff protection during the early stages to support for research and development at the later stages. All these economies have relatively well-developed engineering industries capable of supplying low-cost inputs to electronics manufacturers. They have competitive component supply firms. They were also effective in international marketing strategies. However, ASEAN countries are technologically behind Hong Kong, Korea, and Taiwan.

Until 1980, the share of Japanese worldwide investments in electrical industries was 12.6 percent of total Japanese foreign investment (Tanaka, 1993). The corresponding share in Asia was 11.9 percent. Between 1981 and 1985, there was a drastic change. Whereas the share of the electrical industries in Asia was reduced to 9.8 percent, it rose to 18.3 percent globally for Japanese companies. Between 1986 and 1990, these two shares converged again at a level of about 30 percent. Foreign direct investment in Asia by the Japanese electrical industries followed the same pattern established by overall Japanese manufacturing investments until 1980; after that period, the level of investments in the Asian electrical industries by Japan was very low. Before 1964, the share of Asia in total Japanese investments in electrical industries worldwide was 83.3 percent. During the second half of the 1960s, the share was reduced to 56.8 percent due mainly to the investments in Latin America. Later, there were investments in North America as well, and the share of Asia during the early 1970s was 48.8 percent. During the later half of 1970s, the share of Asia was further reduced to 30.8 percent, whereas the share of North America was increased to 48.5 percent, which went up further during the early 1980s to 67 percent. The share of Europe was also increased and the share of Asia was reduced further to 14.5 percent. During the latter part of 1980s, the share of Asia was increased to 20 percent.

Investments by the Japanese electrical industry in Asia up to the 1960s were mainly in ASEAN and Taiwan. In ASEAN countries, due to their import-substitution policy introduced during the 1960s, Japan could no longer export profitably. Thus, in order to jump the tariff wall, Japanese companies had to invest. For a similar reason, investments in Latin America went up. Investments in Taiwan increased due to a different reason. There the labor costs were much lower at that time, so having their production bases for reexport was profitable for Japanese companies. Since the 1970s, the Asian countries, instead of import-substitution policies, have started export-promotion policies and Japanese companies have taken advantage of their low labor cost to reexport from their production bases in those countries. It was first started with Taiwan and Korea, then Singapore and Malaysia gained importance. In the latter part of 1970s, Singapore became the most important overseas production base for Japanese multinationals. Increasing trade conflicts due to Japanese export drives and the corresponding threats of tariffs and other trade restrictions from the developed countries provoked investments in North America. Japanese companies have increased their direct investments in both North America and Europe in order to avoid trade frictions and tariff walls (mainly in Europe).

Investments by the Japanese electrical industry, both in the Asian NIEs and in ASEAN, account for a little less than 30 percent of the total manufacturing investments of Japanese origin. In the Asian NIEs, the electrical industry shares the same fate as the manufacturing industry regarding investments, that is, there are downward tendencies after 1988. In the ASEAN, Thailand and Malaysia have received the largest share of foreign investments, which has followed the pattern set by the manufacturing sector with high levels of investments. Investments in Singapore were at a low level after 1988. In the Philippines, they rose to a high level in 1990, but soon declined.

Multinational Companies in the ASEAN Semiconductor Industry

Multinational companies are most active in semiconductors (Table 5.1). Malaysia has about seventeen multinational corporations (a dozen of them are from the United States) with semiconductor assembly/test operations. Singapore has fourteen semiconductors-oriented multinationals, a few with circuit-design and wafer-fabrication facilities besides many with assembly and testing alone. The Philippines has a dozen assembly/testing facilities operated by multinationals in addition to several local assembly plants. Thailand also has similar facilities. Indonesia has a few as well. The first wave of investments took place when the U.S. firms began setting up offshore assembly plants. A series of investments in Malaysia followed these investments, so that by the mid-1970s Malaysia became the leading offshore assembly location. A few investments occurred in Indonesia, the Philippines, and Thailand in the mid-1970s. In the Philippines, the industry took off when U.S. multinationals made rapid investments. By 1983, the Philippines had overtaken Singapore in terms of semiconductor exports to the United States. However, due to political uncertainties in the Philippines, semiconductor companies are looking elsewhere—possibly to Thailand—for future expansion of their capacities. Indonesia has failed to attract semiconductor investment due to complications relating to imports of raw materials, exports of the finished products, and an underdeveloped infrastructure to cover the needs of export-oriented firms.

There are fears that the rate of expansion of offshore assembly operations by semiconductor firms will be slower in the near future than in the past due to existing automatic assembly plants. Any future investments in new plants will involve the most advanced automated assembly equipment. There is a greater tendency now to find new assembly plants close to final markets. Many of the Japanese semiconductor firms have pursued a market-oriented assembly strategy to mitigate trade frictions and protectionist pressures within the major foreign markets for Japanese semiconductors. That was particularly true in the United States and Europe. However, there is another possibility. Developing Asia has become a rapidly growing market for semiconductor devices. Electronics firms in Asian NIEs have become world leaders in the export of a variety of consumer electronics products as well as certain types of computer peripherals and communication equipment. All these products incorporate semiconductor devices of various types in varying quantities. U.S. multinational companies manufacturing microcomputers and peripherals, calculators, and certain communication equipments have been investing in Asian production facilities in recent years in an effort to remain competitive with low-cost hardware obtained from Japan or Asian NIEs. These have helped to stimulate growth in regional demand for semiconductors. In the short to medium term, U.S. multinationals will depend on their offshore assembly operations since they have virtually no large-scale assembly facilities in the United States. Therefore, firms will continue to depend on their offshore plants for several years to meet the bulk of their assembly needs.

Multinationals in the Consumer Electronics Industry

The consumer-electronics sector of ASEAN countries (except Singapore) developed initially through industries substituting imports. Multinational corporations within this industry, mainly from Japan, have made direct investments to avoid tariffs and other barriers to exports. The most frequent condition imposed by the host countries in the ASEAN was to have a domestic joint-venture partner. In the semiconductor industry, however, no such conditions could have deterred investments. The reason is that the semiconductor industry is primarily for export whereas market penetration was the main objective for foreign direct investments in consumer-electronics sectors.

Table 5.2 demonstrates the ranges of multinational companies investing in consumer-electronics industries in ASEAN regions. In most countries, the bulk of investments was related to the import-substitution policies that occurred in the late 1960s and early 1970s. Singapore was the most successful recipient and Indonesia was the least. Most of the investments in Singapore were export-oriented. Some of these export-oriented industries also have moved to Malaysia because of close geographical relations. There are also some export-oriented schemes in the Philippines due to the ranges of incentives given to the consumer-

Table 5.1

Investments by Major Multinational Semiconductor Corporations in the ASEAN Region

	Indonesia	Malaysia	Phillippines	Singapore	Thailand
Japanese multinationals					
Hitachi		at (3) (1973)		at (3)	
Matsushita				at (2) (1978)	
NEC		at (1) (1974)		at (1976)	
Toshiba					
U.S.-based multinationals					
Advanced Micro Devices		at (1)	at (1) (1977)	td	at (1) (1984)
American Microsystems Inc (AMI)			at (1)		
AT&T					at (1) (1984)
Data General			at (1) (1978)		at (1) (1974)
Fairchild	a (1)		at (1)	atd	
General Instrument		at (1)			
GM (DELCO)				at	
Harris		at (1)	at (1)		
Hewlett-Packard		at (1)		atd	
Intel		at (1)	at (1) (1974)		
Intersil				at (1)	
Monolithic Memories		at (1)			
Mostek		at (2)			
Motorola		aat (2)	at (1) (1979)		
National Semiconductor	a (1)	at (2)	at (1) (1`976)	at	at (1) (1973)
RCA		aat (1)			

Signetics				at (1) (1974)
Silicon Systems Inc.			atd	
Synertec			atd	at (1980)
Texas Instruments	at (1)	at (1)	at	
Western Digital	at (1)			
Zilog		at (1) (1979)		
Western Europe multinationals				
AEG-Telefunken		at (1) (1974)		
Philips		a (1)		
Siemens	at (2)			
SGS-SAtes	at (1)			
Thomson-CSF			t	

Note: a = assembly; t = testing; d = design; number of plants in first brackets; startup date in second brackets.
Source: UNCTAD

electronics sector. The bulk of these investments in the region, however, was geared to the domestic market. In a few instances when the host country required that foreign investors meet local-content requirements, foreign companies built large-scale facilities for the manufacture of particular components in order to export excess amounts that the market of the host country could not absorb. For example, a multinational company manufacturing television sets in Malaysia supplies flyback transformers to its other television manufacturing plants in the region. Some import-substituting television manufacturing units in the region have begun to export electrolytic capacitors, tuner subassemblies, and so on. Similarly, multinationals use their feeder plants to supply components and subassemblies to a regional chassis or final assembly plant producing television sets for export. For chassis assembly, the output is generally destined for the U.S. market, since the duty structure of the United States favors imports of chassis-level assemblies for final assembly within the United States.

There are a number of companies from various developing countries that are having joint-venture partnerships with local companies in the ASEAN area. Although this feature is not restricted to the consumer-electronics sector alone, it is very common in this sector. Original Equipment Manufacturer's (OEM) agreements are also common features of the consumer-electronics industry in these countries. An electronics firm's market share in a particular country may be too small to justify the establishment of its own production facilities to serve that market; trade barriers may render exporting to that market uneconomic as well. Under these circumstances, the firm can arrange with another firm already established in the market to devote part of its capacity of making color television sets on an OEM basis to be sold under the original firm's brand name. Many television manufacturers in ASEAN countries have surplus capacities, so these arrangements normally prove beneficial to the firms involved. There can be another explanation. A multinational company, for example, may have limited capacity in its existing facilities to manufacture all the products demanded by the market. Rather than constructing a new facility, it can ask for a contract with another multinational company in a nearby country to absorb some of its orders, mainly for low-value-added items. This will allow the company to concentrate on its high-value-added products. There are many reasons why Singapore was successful in developing consumer-electronics industries, whereas others are not. There is a lack of supporting industries and reli-

Table 5.2

Investments by Major Multinational Consumer Electronics Companies

Company	Indonesia	Malaysia	Philippines	Singapore	Thailand
Japan-based					
Aiwa				RC	
Akai			X		
Asahi Electronics			X	TR, TA	
Clarion		CR			
Dauhatsu				R, RC	
Foster Electric				HF	
Hitachi			X	T, R, TR	
JVC				HF	
Matsushita Electric	T, R, (70)	T	T	R, RC, TR	T, R, RC (69)
Mistubishi				T, R	
Sanyo	X (69)		X	R, RC	T, T, (70)
Sharp		T, RC	X		
Toshiba		T		T	T (70)
Toyo Electronics		R			
Trio Kenwood				HF	
U.S.-based					
General Electric		T, R, RC			
GM				CM	
ITT		R, RC			
Western Europe-based					
Philips		R			
Thomson Brandt		T			

Note: T = television sets; TA = telephone answering machine; R = radio; RC = radio cassette recorders; CR = car radio; TR = tape recorders; HF = hi-fidelity audio equipment; X = nature of operation not specified
Source: UNCTAD

able suppliers in other countries in this region. Whereas Singapore can supply everything from its local base, from plastic moldings to metal stampings, it has a distinct cost advantage in forgings and precision machined parts.

Japanese Investments in Asia in the Consumer-Electronics Sector

The number of Japanese overseas subsidiaries in Asia had two peaks. The first peak for foreign investments in Asian NIEs was in Taiwan in the late 1960s and later it was extended to Korea and Hong Kong in early 1970s. The second peak was in both Taiwan and Korea during the late 1980s. In the ASEAN, the first peak was from the early 1970s; in Singapore and Malaysia, it was up to the late 1970s. The second peak was from 1987 to 1989 in Thailand and in 1990 in Malaysia. These profiles parallel the corresponding activities of Japanese overseas investments in the electronics industry in Asia. However, there are some important differences as well. Japanese investments in Malaysia were made by industries manufacturing electronics parts primarily as a reaction to investments in ASEAN semiconductor industries by the United States. Investments in Asian NIEs were not as large as they were in the ASEAN during the peak investment period of the late 1980s. Investments in Asian NIEs were a response to the appreciation of the exchange rate of the yen and were made by small companies manufacturing electronics parts that set up their operations in a short period. The Japanese consumer-electronics industries, in response to the strong yen, have invested in the ASEAN countries after 1987 and the manufacturing units of these industries have moved there after a few years. There was thrust of direct investments from Japan to the ASEAN region since the late 1980s. These are concentrated in certain areas.

Between 1986 to 1990, 55 percent of new Japanese electronics companies are located in Malaysia and Thailand. In the consumer-electronics sector, 62 percent of new Japanese companies are in Malaysia and Thailand. The ASEAN has received 68 percent of the new Japanese companies in the entire electronics industry and 80 percent of the new Japanese companies in the consumer-electronics sector. Considering the volume of Japanese investments during the same period for the entire electronics industry, 73 percent went to Malaysia and Thailand. For the consumer-electronics sector, Malaysia and Thailand have received 72 percent of Japanese investments. In that sector, investments were aimed at taking advantages of the low labor costs in those countries rather than to avoid the consequences of the strong yen. The decision to have their export bases in the ASEAN countries was made before 1985. The subsequent appreciations of the yen have only intensified the decisions of Japanese companies. There was a risk of escalating procurement costs for parts if raw materials and components would come from Japan and the local subsidiaries would only do the assembly. In order to have a stable cost of production, increasing shares of locally made components were necessary. Producers of parts thus went to those countries in response to the needs of the finished-goods producers from Japan. Thus, supply-chain networks are formed for Japanese subsidiaries within

ASEAN. We can call it a horizontal integration between Japan and the ASEAN.

Multinational Companies in the Industrial-Electronics Industry

Table 5.3 shows investments made by major multinational companies in the industrial-electronics sector in the ASEAN area. There are many Western European companies in this sector, but they are not well represented in the other electronics sectors. The roles of Japanese companies are somehow limited in this sector reflecting their preference for Japan-based production in highly automated facilities. As we have seen in the case of consumer-electronics sectors, there are two types of investments in this sector: (a) import-substituting type, that is, to supply telecommunications equipment to national telecommunications authorities, and (b) export-promotion efforts, that is, in production of computer peripherals like disk drives, printers, keyboards, personal computer central-processing units or subassemblies, and telephone and mobile-radio subscriber equipment. In the first category, public sectors in the host countries have directly encouraged joint-sector-equity participation and local-content requirements are part of the conditions for entry. In the second category, the price advantages maintained by the Japanese and Asian NIE competitors in their home countries have provoked Western multinationals to transfer their production bases to the ASEAN area. For cordless telephones, a large share of the U.S. market is now captured by the imports from Hong Kong and Taiwan. These types of export-oriented projects went mainly to Singapore and Malaysia. In fact, Singapore is one of the largest exporters of computer disk drives in the world. Malaysia is one of the leading exporters of pocket pagers and mobile two-way radio units. Thailand and Malaysia both have attracted significant investments in computer peripherals production. However, both Indonesia and the Philippines are marginal producers in this area; uncertain investment climates and lack of supply networks are the prominent reasons for the low level of participation by multinationals in these two countries.

Multinationals in the Nonsemiconductor-Components Industry

Table 5.4 lists investments in other electronics components manufactured or assembled by foreign multinational companies in ASEAN countries. Some component production by multinationals is vertically

Table 5.3

Investments by Major Multinational Industrial Electronic Companies in ASEAN

	Indonesia	Malaysia	Philippines	Singapore	Thailand
Japan-based					
Fujitsu				PS	
Mineba				KB, PR	KB
NEC		TS, PS		SF	
Soar Electronics				DM	
U.S. and Canada-based					
Apple Computer				PC	
Applied Magnetics				MH	
AT&T				TS	
Computer Memories				DD	
Data General				MN, SF	
Digital Equipment				MN	
Foxboro				IC	
GTE Industries			X		
Hewlett-Packard				CL, AI, TM SF, PR, PC	
ITT					TS
King Radio				MT	
Maxtor				DD	
Mentor Graphics				CW	
Microscience				DD	
Miniscribe				DD	
Motorola Communications		CR, EP		EP, CR	
Northern Telecom		TS			
Printronix				PR	
Seagata				DD	DH
Tandon				DD	
Taylor Instruments				IC	
Texas Instruments			CL		
Western Europe-based					
Robert Bosch		AE			
EB Communications				MT	
Ericsson		PS, PX, MR			
Lucas		AE			
Marconi		ML			
Nixdorf Computer				Pr, KB	
Oliveti				ET, PR	
Philips				PX	

Note: AE = automotive electronics; AI = analytical instruments; CL = calculators; CR = cellular radios; CW = computer workstations; DD = disk drives; DH = disk heads; DM = digital multimeters; EP = electronic pagers; ET = electronic typewriters; IC = industrial controls; KB = keyboards; MF = mainframe; MH magnetic heads; ML = multiplex equipment; MN = minicomputers; MR = mobile radios; MT = maritime transceivers; PC = personal computers; PR = printers; PS = public switching equipment; PX = private branch exchanges; SF = software; TD = tape drives; TM = test and measurement equipment; TS = telephone sets; X = not specified.

Source: UNCTAD

linked to the final assembly of electronics equipments for the domestic market. Other production is for exports or for the parent company or another subsidiary. In general, components produced in ASEAN plants are normally using labor-intensive methods. Singapore is an exception because it has a substantial amount of component production linked to the growth of its export-oriented electronics equipment industry. Cost controls over materials and labor was the key for investments in Singapore. The proximity of component suppliers to customers has been a primary consideration as well.

In the last few years, most electronics companies from various developing countries have developed subcontracting manufacturers and assemblers for multinationals from the developed countries. Some of these companies are in joint ventures with well-known manufacturers from the developed countries providing both technology and goodwill. Table 5.5 lists such enterprises. Most of these companies are from Hong Kong or Taiwan and they have close contact with the Chinese enterprises in the host ASEAN countries. Singapore has received many such investments, and at the same time has invested in Malaysia and Indonesia. As the electronics industries in Asian NIEs upgrade their products and technology of production, and as the standard of living and wage rates in those countries rise, multinationals involved in electronics will transfer their production bases to low-wage countries such as China, Bangladesh, and Sri Lanka.

Japanese Multinationals and Japan–ASEAN Trade

For Japanese foreign subsidiaries, exports to Japan and Third World countries are more important. Although local sales in the ASEAN were important in certain sectors, sales to Japan were prominent features. Exports from the electrical machinery sector to Japan have a share of 18 percent of total sales. For natural resources and food industries, the corresponding shares were much greater. However, in sectors involving higher levels of technology, the shares of Third World countries in total sales are more important than sales to Japan and to the local markets of the host countries. This proves that although ASEAN countries have encouraged Japanese companies to invest in import-substituting industries, gradually these subsidiaries became important export bases for Japanese parent companies.

In the case of TVs and VCRs from Thailand and Malaysia to Japan,

Table 5.4

Investments by Multinationals in the Nonsemiconductor Component Industries in ASEAN

	Indonesia	Malaysia	Philippines	Singapore	Thailand
Japan-based					
CMK				PC	
Dai-Ichi Electronics					
Fujitsu	MS		RL		
Hokuriku				RS	
Japan Servomotors				MM	
Kami Electronics				TR	
Kisho Electronics				CM	
Koa Denko	RS				
Kyodo Electronics				PS, TR	
Matsushita	CA, FT		CA		
Meiden Quartz				CR, OS	
Minibea				TR	MM
Mitsui Hi-Tech				LF	
Mitsumi		TR	X	CL	
Murata				FL, CA, RS	
Nemic-Lambda				PS	
Nichikon				CA	
Orim Manufacturing				MM	
Rybycon				CA	
Sankyo Seiki				MM, MH	
SEH		SW			
Sumida Electric				TR, AN, CL	
Taiyo Yuden				CA	
Tamura		TR			
Tanaka Electronics				BW	
Tanashin				CM	
Yokohama Magnetic				MH	

the value of exports to Japan was not important, but in the case of air conditioners and refrigerators that value was quite prominent. However, one can look at these values from Japan's viewpoint. Total imports (U.S. dollar basis) to Japan were increased by 1.8 times between 1985 to 1991. Imports of consumer electricals were increased by 11.7 times, but the imports from the ASEAN countries of consumer-electrical products were increased by 17.2 times. The share of Asia in consumer electricals rose from 47 percent in 1985 to 69 percent in 1991. For household electrical appliances, about 71 percent imports were from Asia in 1991.

Total amount of imports from the Asian NIEs and the ASEAN of consumer-electrical appliances were ¥145.3 billion in 1989. It increased to ¥177.2 billion in 1991. The share of these two regions in total imports

Table 5.4 *(continued)*

	Indonesia	Malaysia	Philippines	Singapore	Thailand
U.S.-based					
Allen Bradley				RS, FR, HC	
American Fine Wire				BW	
AMP				CN	
Corning Glass				CA	
CTS Corp.				RS, OS, HC	
Du Pont				CN	
Cynacraft (National Semiconductor)		IF	IF		
Faraday				CA	
Litton Components				SL	
Molex				CN, IS	
Monsanto		SW			
Western Europe-based					
Demerton				BW	
E. Hort				CA, CL	
Pentex-Schweizer				PC	
Pepperl & Fuchs				MS	
Seiments Components CTS Corp.				CA, CL, FR	
Welke Top Heads GmbH				CN	

Notes: AN = antennas, BW = bonding wire, CA = capacitors, CL = coils, CM = cassette mechanisms , CN = connectors, CR = crystals, CS = ceramic substrates, CT = cathode ray tubes, FL = filters, FR = ferrites, FT = flyback transformers, HC = hybrid circuits, IS = IS sockets, IF = lead frames, LS = loudspeakers, MH = magnetic heads, MM = micro motors, MS = micro switches, OS = oscillators, PC = printed circuit boards, PS = power supplies, RL = relays, RS = resistors, SL = solder, SP = speakers, SW = silicon wafers, TR = transformers, SW = watch modules, X = nature of operation not specified.

Sources: based on company publications, directories of manufacturers, and investment boards

went up from 68 to 74 percent during that period. However, when the imports from the ASEAN area were increased by 8.12 times, imports from the Asian NIEs were reduced. As a result, the ratio of imports from Asian NIEs and the ASEAN became 53:47 in 1991 from 93:7 in 1989. Thus, imports from the ASEAN area have become just as important as those from the Asian NIEs. The effect of decreased imports and increased exports with the Asian NIEs and increased exports and imports with the ASEAN was noticed in household electronics, audiovisual equipment, and white goods. For white goods such as refrigerators, air conditioners, and electric washing machines, the ASEAN countries have already replaced the Asian NIEs as exporter to Japan. In the case of less-value-added items such as electric shavers, electric fans, and vacuum cleaners,

Table 5.5

Foreign Direct Investments in the ASEAN Region by Electronics Firms Based in Developing Countries

Investor firm	Home country	Indonesia	Malayasia	Philippines	Singapore	Thailand
Atlas Electronics	Hong Kong		Atlas/Intek Atlas Electronics		Aiwa/Atlas Electronics	
Conic Electronics	Hong Kong	Pte Ltd.			Conic Electronics	
Multi Tech	Taiwan		Joint Ventures Planned			
Printed Circuits International	Hong Kong				Printed Circuits International Pte Ltd.	
Roxy Electric	Hong Kong		Roxy Electric Industries Sharp-Roxy		Roxy Electric Industries	
Rubina Watch Assembling Co., Ltd.	Singapore	Rubina Watch Assembl. Indonesia Ltd.				
Singatronics Singapore Pte Ltd.	Singapore		Singatronics Sdn. Bhd			
Tatung	Taiwan				Tatung Electronics	
Wearne Brothers	Singapore		JR Electronics Sdn. Bhd.			

Sources: Based on company interviews; *New Strait Times* and *Business Times* (Malaysia); directories of manufacturers/exporters; and UNCTAD

imports from the Asian NIEs are either decreasing or remaining constant. That is also the case for imports of black-and-white television sets. These shifts toward the ASEAN for high-value-added items were promoted and maintained by Japanese foreign subsidiaries. Japanese parent companies try to create some networks of international work sharing among its subsidiaries. According to this strategy, the Asian NIEs would produce goods with low value added, demands for which are either constant or decline. The ASEAN area was chosen as the producers of high-value-added items by introducing the latest technologies for mass production and with quality superior to those produced by the Asian NIEs. Japanese consumers prefer high-quality goods, which can be produced in Japan, whereas foreign subsidiaries can produce goods to satisfy the demands of foreign countries in a region where labor costs are low and where Japanese supply networks either are well-established or can be developed quickly. This has a dual effect. Japanese supply networks can maintain the competitive position in the home market by developing new products with improved qualities. Goods produced in the foreign subsidiaries at much lower production costs can be exported worldwide. The export to Japan of such products produced in foreign subsidiaries may be difficult because of the shifts of home demands toward goods with higher quality.

Conclusion

It is possible that the ASEAN region will receive investments in offshore assembly plants manufacturing semiconductors, but the rate of growth of investments in the ASEAN area is likely to decline. This negative rate of growth can be compensated for by the fact that East and Southeast Asia are becoming markets for semiconductors. Just as Japanese firms have successfully challenged some Western competitors, some firms from the Asian NIEs are now challenging Japanese firms in the lower end of consumer-electronics market (e.g., radios, television sets, digital watches, and calculators). Some of these Asian NIE firms have also entered the high end of the market (e.g., video recorders). It is possible that in the future, the Japanese firms will lose market shares to these firms from the Asian NIEs and instead focus their attention to industrial electronics. Japanese consumer-electronics firms will concentrate more on product innovations and quality improvement as they can no longer compete on pricing.

The technology to produce low-value-added electronics products such as radios or black-and-white TV sets are easily available, so technological complexity is not a deterrent for entry by firms from the ASEAN region. However, the multinational corporations in consumer electronics continue to dominate most markets of the ASEAN region largely because of their managerial and marketing advantages. One of the principal explanations for the cost disadvantages faced by local producers is the lack of proper suppliers of materials and components. Thus, even in a joint venture with a local manufacturer, a multinational company can gain only under a market protected by tariff and other nontariff restrictions. So it is almost impossible for local producers of the ASEAN to compete in the international market for low-value-added electronics products against the Asian NIEs.

In the industrial-electronics sector, except for Singapore, all other countries have invested in the domestic market in products such as telephone subscriber equipment, cellular radio units, and computer peripherals. Because these industries depend heavily on precision engineering for parts and components, such industries can be located in countries that have a qualified work force and a precision components industry. Singapore is successful in this sector. Others are quite weak. Thus, any multinational company willing to invest in this sector has to develop necessary supply-chain networks to maintain controls over the quality of the product.

So far, investments in computer manufacturing sectors except Singapore are very limited. The bulk of the production is still performed within developed countries. Most multinationals have chosen Hong Kong, Korea, Singapore, and Taiwan for these industries mainly because of the availability of adequate engineering support and supply networks. Often, the multinationals do not manufacture there, but provide support to a local manufacturer on an OEM (Original Equipment Manufacturer) basis. Generally, such multinationals have reluctantly agreed to less-than-full-equity ownership as a condition for entering a market that would be closed otherwise. China, Mexico, and Korea are some examples. In the case of Korea, the local joint-venture partners have expertise to undertake difficult technical and managerial tasks. No comparable inducements exist in the ASEAN area so far. Recently, there are some investments in joint ventures in Taiwan and Malaysia. Unless there is trade protection for domestic producers, including multinationals, they need to export a major part of their production to the international market as their domestic market is large enough to create necessary economics of scale in production.

In the nonsemiconductor sector, the degree of precision required varies from product to product. In the case of industrial electronics, the degree of precision required is very high. That is possibly the reason that most multinational investments in the ASEAN area are in the consumer-electronics sector. Also, for many electronics products, the life cycle from the first commercial production to obsolescence has been reduced from a few years to a few days. We do not expect ASEAN countries to manufacture state-of-the-art products, except through the total reliance on multinationals from developed countries. Even relatively mature products have such a short lifespan that profitable investments by ASEAN domestic companies will be impossible. The problem of product obsolescence has not created a serious problem so far, because in the ASEAN, multinational companies completely dominate their subsidiaries regarding manufacturing and marketing. In semiconductor industries in the ASEAN, their operations, namely, assembly and testing, are not affected by rapid obsolescence because these can be converted to the assembly of new device types.

The real question is whether local manufacturers in the ASEAN area can sell products to the international market that are designed and developed indigenously. There is another issue. Increasing automation of production processes in the electronics sector by the multinationals has created an increasing demand for highly skilled electronics technicians and engineers. The shortages of local supplies of such a labor force can create a serious constraint in the future. Automation is not induced by the increasing cost of low-level labor, but by the complexities of the production process in most electronics sectors and by the desire to reduce the costs of materials, which is the most important part of the production cost in the electronics sector as a whole. In order to ensure quality and reliability, microprocessor controlled assembly equipment is now indispensable. The final assembly system, particularly in subsidiaries of Japanese multinationals, is integrally linked to some version of the just-in-time inventory method. Conservation on use, reduction of waste during production, and reduction on inventories during production can save a large part of material cost.

Japanese multinationals are worried about the dominance of American multinationals in the ASEAN area. Japanese multinationals have achieved price competitiveness without extensive reliance on low-cost offshore assembly operations in electronics sectors. If they use highly automated home-based production and succeed in forcing U.S. multinationals out of certain semiconductors and computer markets, the long-term consequences can be a termination of certain ASEAN operations by the multinational electronics firms. In Singapore, certain U.S. multinationals have already curtailed their operations in disk-drive manufacturing due to intense competition from Japanese manufacturers. Similarly, in Malaysia, another U.S. multinational manufacturing random-access memories (RAMs) has reduced its production levels due to Japanese competitions.

Certain Japanese multinationals in the semiconductors sector are exporting to the United States from their ASEAN bases. Since exports to the United States or Europe from the ASEAN do not add to Japan's trade surplus on semiconductors with the United States or Europe, it was hoped that trade friction between Japan and the Western developed countries would not arise and that could have induced more Japanese investments in the ASEAN. However, that strategy has not worked well. Japan is exporting to Europe from its bases in Scotland and Ireland. In the United States, Japanese companies are establishing semiconductor assembly and testing facilities in order to reduce the trade friction between Japan and the United States.

If the electronics industries in the ASEAN region are to progress from assembly to integrated production and indigenous technological developments, dramatic improvement in the technology base and absorption capacity is needed. Such improvement should not be confined to the electronics sector only, since this sector is linked to a number of upstream supplier industries and downstream user industries. Without improvement in metalworking, plastic molding, precision machining, and so on, the prospects for the development of electronics-equipment industries are limited. Without improvement in the manufacturing process of equipment, the prospects for development of the component industries are limited as well.

Appendix: Method of Estimation

Definition

(1) Export substitution effect = (sales of locally incorporated enterprises) × (1 – ratio of sales to Japan) × Japan's share

Japan's share = (value of world imports from Japan in the *i*th industry) / total value of world imports in the *i*th industry

(2) Export inducement effect = intermediate goods exports (compensated purchases of locally incorporated enterprises × ratio of imports from Japan to purchases) + capital goods exports (plant and equipment investments of locally incorporated enterprises × ratio of imports from Japan to plant and equipment investments)

(3) Imports from locally incorporated enterprises' effect = (sales of locally incorporated enterprises) × (ratio of sales to Japan to total sales)

(4) Import conversion effect = sum of increases and decreases of domestic production caused by the preceding (1) to (3)

In order to estimate these effects, the Input–Output Table of Japan, 1991, was used. The method used is as follows:

$$M_i = m_i (A_{ij}X_j + Y_i) \qquad (1)$$

where m_i = *i*th row of M (import) matrix, m_i = import coefficient vector *i*th industry; A = input coefficient matrix; X = domestic production matrix; Y = domestic final-demand vector; and *i*, *j* = dimensions of the input–output matrix, representing various industries.

The supply-demand balance identity is

$$A \times X + F - M = X \qquad (2)$$

The final demand is divided into domestic final demand *Y* and export demand *E*.

$$F = Y + E \qquad (3)$$

Thus, by substituting (3) into (2), we get

$$A \times X + Y + E - M = X \qquad (4)$$

We can rewrite (1) as

$$M = m\,(A \times X + Y) \qquad (5)$$

Substituting (5) into (4), we get

$$A \times X + Y + E - m\,(A \times X + Y) = X \text{ or } [I - (1 - m)\,A]X = (1 - m)Y + E \text{ or } X = (\text{Inverse of } [I - (1 - m)A]) \times [(1 - m)Y + E] \qquad (6)$$

We can compute the impact on domestic production (X) by putting increases and decreases of exports and imports caused by the export inducement effect, the export substitution effect, and the import inducements effect from locally incorporated firms into (6).

Impacts on employment can be obtained by using the formula

$$LL = L \times X$$

(where L = labor requirement matrix and LL = employment vector) to obtain changes in employments due to any changes in production as obtained from (6).

6

ASIAN ECONOMIC CRISIS AND THE ROLE OF JAPAN

The purpose of this chapter is to analyze present economic conditions in some important Asian countries considering their current economic crisis and ongoing economic reforms. Although East Asian economies have experienced rapid economic growth in recent years, since 1995, slower world demands have created lower rates of economic growth. A combination of adverse currency movements and weak demands in the industrialized world, particularly for electronics goods, continues to upset Asia's export prospects and therefore, economic growth. That, in turn, is raising the debate whether the region's economic growth can be sustained. Across the region, the strains are starting to show, particularly after the recent currency crisis in 1997–1998. In South Korea, exports fell in 1995 for the first time in many years. Chinese manufacturers are mentioning the VAT rebates and the credit squeeze for the 8.2 percent drop in exports. For South Korea, whose exports of cars and finished electronics compete with Japan, this has been a particular setback. For China, the dollar's rise means a real appreciation in its own currency. Between 1994–1996, the Chinese yuan had moved to 8.3 to the dollar from 8.7, but China has had much higher inflation. Experience shows that a rise in the real exchange rate affects exports very quickly. For Singapore, from the recent experience, a 1 percent rise in the exchange rate means a 1.7 percent fall in exports. Thailand and the Philippines have seen the fastest real rise in their exchange rates recently. However, productivity gains can neutralize much of the real appreciation. In some countries, however, wage costs are rising faster than productivity; Malaysia is an example. Southeast Asian countries depend on their electronics exports until now and weakness of the electronics market due to the collapse in semiconductor prices and the slow personal computer market in Europe are aggravating factors. Indonesia, Thailand, and Malaysia all have large balance-of-payments deficits that must be financed by capital inflows. Some large parts of these inflows are attracted by relative yields; if global interest rates stay the same and the exchange-rate risk premiums go up, local interest rates have to rise. With the exception of China with its large reserves and current account surplus, most Asian countries cannot easily afford the uncertainty that would flow from allowing their currencies to depreciate.

Weakness in export markets has focused attention on whether Malaysia and Thailand have the capacity to move into more sophisticated, higher-value manufacturing. Hong Kong used to make its earnings from textiles; now it makes it from financial services. Thailand is already beginning to follow suit. However, Thai policy makers are worried how far their country, which has no long tradition of compulsory secondary education, can travel down this road. Thailand and Malaysia are not quite at the top end of technology and they do not have the skilled labor. They also do not have cost advantages like Indonesia can offer.

Despite strong regional growth, Asian manufacturers are still dependent on the markets in developing countries, which makes economic adjustment painful when global demand falls. Purchasing power is rising in Asia, but it is still far behind that in the Western developed countries, which are the ultimate buyers of what Asia produces.

In the financial sector, though savings rates are generally high, domestic financial markets are underdeveloped and lack the sophistications of intermediate funds of large volumes. Bond markets are in their infancy. Equity markets are often thin and nonliquid. Both lack the stabilizing presence of large institutional investors such as pension funds and insurance companies. To meet the challenge, Asia's financial markets must develop at breakneck speed over the next few years. Change will be spurred by the need for capital and investment requirements of an emerging middle-class country seeking to provide for its old age. Yet these driving forces may clash with the inability of markets to adopt and thus delay in developing appropriate regulatory structures. With their close relations to industrial entrepreneurs, commercial banks are also well placed to control the pace with which new investment banking instruments are introduced.

There are many reasons why Asia has such an underdeveloped financial market. Most Asian governments have substantial budget surpluses and do not need to borrow funds—unlike the United States, Europe, and Japan, which boast large and liquid government bond markets. Where Asian governments do issue bonds, they tend to be nonliquid and are often held by banks and national savings funds with large reserve requirements. Moreover, many countries lack crucial market infrastructures, such as efficient clearing and settlements systems, reliable credit ratings, trading and market-making mechanisms and hedging instruments. Since most private investors in the region are content to lease their money in bank deposits or invest it in their local stock markets, there is a shortage of institutional investors who specialize in buying bonds. However, there are important factors that demand the creation of efficient bond markets in Asian countries. Changing demographic trends and savings patterns have led to the emergence in recent years of investment institutions that require long-term assets, such as insurance companies and pension funds. Another factor is the regions' enormous infrastructure needs, which requires debt of longer maturities than banks are willing to provide. Many Asian countries are also moving from labor-intensive manufacturing to capital-intensive industries, boosting companies' debt financing needs, which require bond financing.

Exchange-listed interest rate derivatives are still in their infancy in Asia. To international investors, Asia's emerging bond markets offer manifold attractions not matched by other emerging markets: attractive yields, high degree of political stability, relatively stable currencies (until recently), and strong economic growth accompanied by relatively moderate inflation rates. International banks can receive excellent rewards in Asia's developing bond markets by benefiting from increased cross-border capital flows, bringing Asian borrowers to the international capital markets, selling non-Asian products into Asia and local-currency bonds to international investors.

There was much optimism for Asia-Pacific equity markets, until the recent turmoils started in 1997. The underlying theme was strong global liquidity. Malaysia had the second largest market after Hong Kong. The government was keen to enhance the stock market's reputation and attract listings from around the world. Opinions on the markets were mixed. Many were bearish in 1996–1997, citing economic risks, although in the very near term, the booming credit conditions, which were helping ignite these risks, would also ensure strong liquidity. Thailand, which has seen share prices go downhill in 1996–1997, was seen by many as a good bet. It had one of the highest rates of earnings per share growth on a three-year view (from 1997) and valuations were likely to rise in tandem with a stronger economy. However, those calculations all went wrong along with the collapse of the Thai currency. Indonesia by contrast had fewer supporters. The government recently was forced to carry political and policy risks, which, combined with the possibility of liquidity-absorbing cash calls, stand to deter foreign investors.

Asian countries are envied throughout the world for their domestic savings rates, which range up to 50 percent, yet collective savings vehicles such as mutual funds or pension funds have been slow to catch on in the region, where most private savings are still kept on deposits with banks or invested directly in the stock market. Strenuous efforts are under way to remedy this; with governments in Hong Kong, Singapore, and Malaysia taking bold steps to liberalize their fund management industries and encourage investors to shift their funds into collective investment pools. So far, investment funds have been slow to catch on. Fewer than 1 percent of Singapore households invest in funds, compared with 4 percent in Hong Kong, more than 10 percent in the UK, and 25 percent in the United States. Another reason funds have not gained much of a following in Asia is that many savers are simply unaware of them. Although 54 percent of Hong Kong's investors were aware of stocks, a mere 7 percent knew what mutual funds are.

For the commercial banker, Asia was the promised land. According to Citicorp, the volume of Asian syndicated credits and floating rate notes, most of which are subscribed by banks, rose to U.S.$81.5 billion in 1995 from U.S.$72.7 billion in 1994. Loan demand remained buoyant thanks to high economic growth rates, and though margins have come under pressure over the years, they were still generally higher than in other parts of the world. The nature of the business has changed from the market's early days in the 1980s, when it was dominated by large credits for sovereign borrowers. Recently, there has been more corporate borrowing and project financing. Sovereign borrowers, who need funds, could raise them in the bond markets. Much more business in aggregate was done in smaller deals for companies not quite large enough to tap the bond markets. This has created a specialized credit market well suited to commercial banks able to carve out relations with such borrowers and analyze credit risk. Since the mid-1990s, economies were overheating in Malaysia, Thailand, and Indonesia. Property prices have been weak in Hong Kong and Taiwan. Chinese banks were burdened with bad loans to state enterprises. However, the international credit market in Asia was relatively free of problems. This was partly because many corporations could finance a large part of their expansion from internally generated cash. The good debt record has reflected a degree of caution among banks, particularly about excessive exposure to volatile property markets. There are risks even today that some companies involved in highly expensive infrastructure projects may become overstretched, creating problems for their bankers.

Increased globalization of the region's foreign-exchange markets are on the way. Several years of heavy capital inflows into the region for direct investment, foreign loans, or portfolio investment have intensified the process of globalizations. G-7 currencies, which have always been actively traded here, are now in a mature market; margins have collapsed and as a result profitability is negligible.

The less liquid Asian currencies still offer more attractive margins for the banks that trade them. Most of the trading is done against the U.S. dollar, although cross-rates, for instance, the Singapore dollar against the Malaysian ringgit are becoming popular. Other currencies are expected to be added to the fast-growing Asian foreign-exchange markets once their governments allow them to become freely convertible: the Chinese renminbi, the Vietnamese dong, the Indian rupee, the South Korean won, and the new Taiwanese dollar. This growing diversity is expected to open lucrative opportunities for banks, which are seeing fewer arbitrage opportunities in the superefficient foreign-exchange markets of the United States and Europe.

Most Asian currencies were not particularly volatile. This was because many of these were pegged, to varying degrees, to the leading G-7 currencies, especially the U.S. dollar. The most controlled currency is the Hong Kong dollar, which has been pegged to the U.S. dollar at a rate of 7.80 since October 1984, and has been trading very close to that level. Indonesia and Thailand's currencies were less tightly managed with the rupiah following a policy of managed depreciation against the dollar of between 4 and 6 percent a year and the baht pegged to a basket of currencies dominated by the dollar and D-marks. Even farther along the spectrum, Singapore followed a managed currency regime but without formal fixings, whereas the Malaysian ringgit and the Philippines peso were the closest to free floating. The stability of Asia's currencies was further cushioned by vast sums of foreign-exchange reserves, which stood at $420 billion for the region at the end of 1995. During 1990 to 1995, most Asian currencies have been confined to a narrow fluctuation band against the U.S. dollar.

By comparison, in Latin America, currencies have depreciated significantly over the same period and devaluation in Argentina, Brazil, and Mexico has been particularly severe and abrupt. However, there was always a possibility that as intraregional trade flows become stronger and the close correlation with the U.S. dollar fades, the pegs could soften and Asia's currencies could become more volatile. When booming growth and increased trade flows continued to drive Asia's currencies into uncharted territory, no amount of central bank intervention could enable currencies to ignore the fundamental driving them.

A country is classified (according to the indicators used by the World Bank) as severely indebted if the ratio of the present value (PV) of debt to the GNP exceeds 80 percent and the ratio of the present value to current (external) receipts (exports of goods and services) exceeds 220 percent. There are two countries in Asia, the Philippines and Indonesia, that are approaching that limit, whereas Thailand and Malaysia are in the same category as Mexico, the country that has suffered a lot due to turmoils of its external accounts. Although the absolute volume of the present value of debts of Malaysia and Philippines are less than that of South Korea and China, Indonesia's debts are much larger than that of China. If we consider the ratio of total debt to GNP, the Philippines, Indonesia, Malaysia, and Thailand are in worse positions compared to India, China, or South Korea. However, the factor that causes much volatility of the foreign-exchange rate of a country's currency is the extent of the short-term debts. The ratio of short-term debts to total external debt is 29.8 percent for Malaysia, 14.3 percent for the Philippines, 43.1 percent for Thailand, 23.1 percent for Indonesia, compared to only 4 percent for India, 16.2 percent for China, 12.65 percent for Argentina, and 20.5 percent for Brazil. The last two countries are the most highly indebted countries in Latin America, so we can see the extent of the problems that the Southeast Asian countries are facing from this comparison.

The conventional wisdom says that as productivity and wages go up in East Asia, so the global center of gravity will shift to other regions where semiskilled labor is plentiful and inexpensive. As the newly industrializing countries, like South Korea and Malaysia, run short of low-cost surplus labor, so they vacate the labor-intensive industry, leaving the way open for Thailand, Vietnam, or India to develop labor-intensive industries. However, in a world of rapidly changing industrial technology, this emphasis on low-cost—invariably low-productivity—labor looks increasingly fragile. One obvious reason for this is the declining importance of direct labor costs in modern manufacturing and the concomitant increase in skill intensities. There is a growing body of evidence to suggest that the lower cost of labor is less important than its quality. If low-cost labor were the key determinant, then many African countries would be attracting East Asian–style levels of foreign investments.

International trade often equalizes labor costs per unit of output, so differences in wages between countries reflect differences in average productivity in their traded sectors. Low wages in developing countries are normally accompanied with low productivity. In 1990, wages in manufacturing in Malaysia were only 15 percent of those in the United States, whereas average productivity in manufacturing was only 15 percent of the United States. This may be due to inferior machinery, infrastructures, and education in poor countries. Increases in productivity should be matched by rising real wages or by a stronger, real exchange rate. Real wages in South Korea, for example, have risen eightfold in dollar terms since 1977. Even with identical technology-developing countries, "productivity will not be up to rich countries" because education and infrastructure are likely to lag behind for many years. Although average unit labor costs in different countries will tend to converge, the productivity gap will vary from one industry to another. In some sectors, such as clothing or consumer electronics, productivity in a developing country may be almost as high as in developed countries, and thus its low wages (determined by average productivity across the whole of manufacturing) will indeed give firms in those industries a cost advantage relative to those in developed countries. In Southeast Asia, labor difficulties are rapidly eroding the region's cost advantage over Western countries. A study conducted by the Political & Economic Risk Consultancy of Hong Kong has indicated various factors that make a country's workforce attractive to foreign investors—including not just the cost of labor, but its quality, availability, and stability. When grades of both skilled and unskilled workers were averaged, only India and the Philippines received high grades. The problems raised by managers vary from country to country. Staff in Hong Kong and Singapore were highly rated for quality, but were expensive and moved from one job to another quickly just as they do in low-cost but poorly skilled Vietnam. In the Philippines, small foreign firms have problems with the workforce because Filipinos appear to respond best when employed by big multinationals with a strong corporate culture. Most companies in Asia complain about the difficulties of finding, training, and keeping employees.

The most striking feature of growth by second-wave Asian "tigers" Indonesia, Malaysia, and Thailand was their success in making the transition from dependence on primary product exports in the 1960s and 1970s to manufactured exports. In all three countries, the share of manufactured exports in total exports grew from 6 percent or less in 1965 to 41 percent in Indonesia, 61 percent in Malaysia, and 77 percent in Thailand by 1992. That was what the already industrialized Asian countries such as Hong Kong, Singapore, South Korea, and Taiwan have experienced when contributions of primary products in exports went down to make room for cars, machinery, drugs, computers, and communication equipment. However, the recent crisis may cause a temporary halt to these activities.

Asian Finance and Equity

Due to high economic growth throughout East and Southeast Asia, demand for funds was enormous. Asian financial markets reflect the attempts made by countries in this region to raise the necessary finance; however, recent experience shows that the allocations of funds in different sectors of the economy are far from optimum. Asian financial markets have recently fallen prey to nervousness at signs of sectoral weakness, caused in Thailand's case by a severe property glut and in the case of South Korea by a collapse of profitability among the country's large companies. There are fears that banking problems could spread, just when a strong financial sector is badly needed. Without it, Asia will have difficulty mobilizing the savings required to finance the infrastructural and industrial development that could sustain its rapid growth rate.

Throughout the region there are questions of how robust are the financial systems. Sharp contraction of growth rates since the early 1990s does not necessarily mean the end of the Asian miracle. The strains through which banks are passing in some countries thus could be seen as an opportunity, rather than a long-term threat to the region's prosperity. There are signs of continuing confidence among leading international banks. Standard Chartered and Citicorp have made excellent profits recently and they have extensive plans for expansion. Although economic growth has slowed, it is still high and continues to be higher than in Latin America or in the industrialized world. Adding to the appeal is a sense that Asia's financial markets are finally becoming more sophisticated, creating opportunities in corporate finance, fund management, and debt issuance. Asia is still a lending market, but the process of securitization is starting to gather pace.

Except China, which has taken advantage of a surge in its own share markets to float a long list of new companies, the economic slowdown in Asia has reduced the flow of new regional equity and privatization issues. The resulting reduction in inflationary pressures seems to stimulate a long-awaited development of the region's bond markets. Asian borrowers have become more active in international debt markets, particularly in the "U.S. bond market" in the United States where several large Asian companies have raised money. For sovereign borrowers, the aim has been to establish a benchmark borrowing from which corporate borrowers can price their own issues. A window of opportunities for such issues was created in recent months by demand from U.S. institutions for higher-yielding paper. Some Asian corporates found it useful to issue long-term debt because equity had become expensive. In the process, they are starting to become more familiar with the idea of debt issuance. Asia's own local currency markets are finally starting to emerge mainly due to the presence of international funds seeking yields. The World Bank and the European Bank for Reconstruction and Development raised funds in Korean won in 1997. The market for eurobonds denominated in Philippine pesos began in 1997 with issues worth some 10 billion pesos. That was followed by a government effort to develop the domestic market with the launch of a 20-year bond.

However, the fear is that uncontrolled offshore markets could make countries vulnerable to crisis that has already occurred. For regional currency markets to offer depth, liquidity, and stability, there is a need for a strong domestic investor base and infrastructure that provides services such as efficient settlement and rating. Asian corporate treasurers are slowly becoming more accustomed to using the capital markets both to raise resources and for liquidity management. However, inefficiency among the region's banks has prevented them from doing so effectively. Quite often, they have taken the route to profits of piling money into property and stock market investments. That has forced many Asian countries to raise resources abroad to finance their industrial development, fueling the external payment's imbalance that is now a source of worry in Thailand and elsewhere.

Many corporations are in a state of transition as they face the next stage of expansion, which often means going overseas. Asian corporates are increasingly seeking credit ratings and many home-grown rating agencies have sprung up to serve their needs within the region. This has enabled more Asian corporations to use the debt markets, where in the recent past they would have automatically issued more equities. Changing dynamics are reflected in the portfolios of investment banks. Fixed income was the single biggest contributor to profits for most investment banks in the region and the base is expected to expand further. The trend toward debt instruments has been further stimulated by greater acceptance, promoted by yield and desire for greater diversification, of Asian paper in the U.S. and European markets. Global bonds placed by Malaysia's national oil company, Petronas, and Reliance of India are some notable examples.

A parallel trend is the growth of domestic bond markets within Asia. Although still thin compared with Europe or the United States, the development of pension schemes in many markets means there will be bigger pools chasing domestic, fixed-income instruments. Asian governments are attempting to put in place the infrastructure needed, particularly about yield curves, issuing paper of ever-increasing maturities to build out the curve, although many governments run balanced budgets and do not need loans.

Bonds are also expected to play a greater role in funding infrastructure projects, following the landmark deal for China's Zhuhai Highway in 1996. Standard & Poor hailed the deal as the first genuine nonresource infrastructure bond issued by a Chinese borrower in the cross-border bond markets. Chase Manhattan Bank is venturing beyond the traditional ground of China and the ASEAN countries and is assessing opportunities in Vietnam and Laos. As well as infrastructure and power, there are petrochemical related projects in Thailand and resource-based projects in Indonesia.

The banking and stock market crisis in Asia is important. The nonperforming loans of banks in Indonesia, Malaysia, the Philippines, Singapore, and Thailand reached the peak by the end of 1998 at U.S.$73 billion or about 14 percent of total outstanding loans. That is equivalent to 13.3 percent of Southeast Asia's gross domestic product, making this downturn more severe than that of Japan in the early 1990s, the U.S. savings and loan crisis of the late 1980s, or any previous setback. Thailand, Malaysia, the Philippines, and Indonesia look particularly vulnerable. Loose regulation, corruption, and overreliance on lending to collapsing property and stock markets all spell trouble. Better regulation will mean stricter imposition of capital requirements, more transparent accounting and disclosure, and better prudential management by regulators to prevent banks running up excessive exposure to the property market.

Asian Equities

Before the dramatic financial crisis of Asia, even in early 1997, demands for capital were huge in the region. Since 1993, when equity capital raising in Asia took off, the most active markets were Hong Kong and China, typically accounting for 30 to 40 percent of volume. In Hong Kong, applications for listings are there from both local and mainland companies. Infrastructures in China remain an important source of demands for funds, with more than $1 billion worth of toll roads in the pipeline. As the capital-raising markets in Asia have flourished, there are now emerging initial public offerings from family held and conglomerates to diversify their businesses into infrastructures to enhance shareholders' value. Examples are Whampoa, the Hong Kong conglomerate, which owns Orange, its UK mobile phone operator, and New World Development, one of the largest property developers in Hong Kong. Hong Kong public companies are capitalizing on strong sentiment to issue more shares, a strategy favored by the red chips or mainland-backed countries, which are the current favorite stocks in Hong Kong. Buyers are influenced by the healthier outlook of China's economy. They also expect more injections of high-quality assets at favorable prices from the parent to the Hong Kong–listed arms.

In 1997, China unveiled the names of thirty-eight companies approved for an overseas listing, the bulk of which are in Hong Kong. Among these companies is Jiangsu Expressway, which is possibly the biggest H share issue. It wanted to raise about U.S.$400 million. The company has a 275-km road linking Nanjing to Shanghai and will be the window company for what is China's wealthiest province after Guangdong. However, in China, the B share markets, theoretically the preserve of foreign investors but in practice traded by most domestic investors, are likely to remain in the shadow of H shares.

Foreign investors prefer the liquidity offered by Hong Kong, Asia's largest market after Tokyo, and the legal environment and disclosure and transparency standards. The Chinese government is trying to improve the lot of B shares by increasing the average size and putting more stress on quality. Thailand and Korea have been among the least active markets in 1997. This was due to investors' skepticism and companies avoiding the raising of capital while valuations were low. The queue of telecom and utility privatization in Thailand was deferred. Malaysia and Singapore had a pessimistic period since 1997, but in Taiwan, the convertible market thrived. Placements or block trades are popular and sectors planning to use the market for cash includes power, energy, and telecom. Indonesia had a number of privatization programs in 1997, from PT Telkom and power issues, although the timing is uncertain. Market strength in the Philippines has not been matched by liquidity. In India, VSN, India's sole international telecom provider, has a successful issue, raising $448 million of international equity. There can be more from India, where disinvestment program is gaining strength.

Fund Management

Deregulation coupled with a growing government awareness of the need for retirement provisions are opening doors across the region. Apart from the traditional centers of Hong Kong and Singapore, Korea is attracting the attention of fund managers. Korea is the ninth largest mutual fund country, but 80 percent of business has been going into bond funds because of high interest rates. China is also opening up. Indonesia now permits fund management joint ventures. Malaysia has so far put forward two proposals, either wholly owned activities, which carry tax advantages, but have restricted scope or joint ventures, which are allowed to engage in local business. Kuala Lumpur is essentially trying to establish itself as a second base for companies already established in Hong Kong. Advantages are a vast population, expanding middle class, political stability, and the opportunity to manage part of the Employee Pension Fund, the country's retirement scheme, which boasts bigger assets than those of Singapore's Central Provident Fund. Disadvantages include tight restrictions on investment and stipulations on the money that can be taken out of the country. Moreover, in response to the Malaysian initiative, Singapore has become more flexible.

Besides deregulation, another big change is forthcoming in Asia in the move toward defined contributions in pension plans. This change will blur the distinction between pension and mutual fund savings.

Bond Markets

The World Bank in a recent analysis (1998) has predicted that the value of paper outstanding in the region was likely to be more than $1,000 billion by 2004 from $338 million in 1994. However, this may be an overestimation. Hong Kong has developed an active and sophisticated debt security market in local currency that can absorb issues with a maturity as long as 10 years, but until recently, there were little signs of serious development elsewhere. In most parts of Asia, the development of domestic bonds remains embryonic. For debt markets to grow in local currency, certain features are essential. Among these are institutional investor bases to provide liquidity, a proper trading infrastructure including settlement systems and transparent information. With many Southeast Asian countries running a balanced budget or fiscal surplus, there is a dearth of benchmark issues from which corporate bonds could be priced. Now, there are tentative signs that the pace of change may be starting to pick up. In 1997, the Philippines issued eurobonds of 10 billion pesos. In 1997, the World Bank and the European Bank for Reconstruction and Development announced issues in Korean won. The Asian Development Bank has also raised funds in Taiwan dollars. China is attempting to develop its domestic bond market for financing infrastructure needs, although these issues remain closed to foreigners. It has also recently announced a plan to allow state enterprises to issue convertible bonds as a prelude to full privatization. Much of the paper is made up of short, dated securities often issued by banks, and in which banks are also often the ultimate end investors. This may change.

Corporate borrowers have started to use the debt markets more, and in some countries, the maturities have been rising. The Malaysian market has seen maturities moving out to 30 years, whereas "five to seven years" are quite common in Indonesian rupiahs. Many investors are still banks. Demand for europeso paper was driven by liquidity in the Philippines banking system. Gradually, international traders are using the currency swap market to attract international investors into some Asian regional issues. Many buyers were attracted by the higher yield on Asian currencies compared with that available on dollars or the Japanese yen. They were prepared to take some currency risks as well. The development of trading suggests that the liquidity base to the secondary market needs to be developed ahead of the primary market. Yet the scale of fixed-income business now starting to develop remains far short of what the World Bank has predicted.

During the Mexico crisis, governments in Asia saw the risk of allowing markets to be developed offshore where they could not be controlled, so they are suspicious of hot money. One concern is that issuing offshore bonds in domestic currency will do little to help develop the domestic market. There are needs for strong domestic markets and institutions like pension funds and insurance companies. Even in Malaysia, where the Employee Provident Fund has a large appetite for paper, an issue can be purchased but then held up to maturity. The present Asian slowdown with its damping effect on inflation may encourage greater investor interest in bonds. The presence of more corporate borrowers suggests family controlled Asian businesses are not quite so reluctant to issue debt as many have previously argued.

The century bond market could prove to have had a short-lived existence in Asia. After a flurry of activity in 1996, the market appears to have turned with the maiden issue from the Philippines central bank being shelved. Interest rates are creeping up, whereas credit spreads are still very tight. With uncertainties over the direction of interest rates, volatility has descended at the long end of the yield curve. The main engines behind the 1996 flurry of activity were historically low interest rates. In this environment, yield-hungry investors sought debt with which they could still feel comfortable, and issuers were prepared to go into the market because rates were low and spreads sufficiently tight. For corporates, century bonds especially are quasi-equity or even cheap equity. For government issuers, bonds benefit the country corporates by establishing pricing benchmarks. Demands for Asian century bonds have been almost exclusively in the United States (although a small proportion of the Reliance Corporation's share of India's debts was distributed in Europe and Asia) and bankers consider the pending changes in the U.S. tax regime will boost demand for Asian paper.

Derivatives

There can be few better symbols of the drive that has helped make Singapore the financial center of Southeast Asia than the Singapore International Monetary Exchange, Simex, the first financial futures market in Asia. Since it was set up in 1984, it has established nineteen international futures and options contracts based on offshore financial derivatives. Singapore's future as a financial center will depend on its ability to meet demand for more sophisticated and innovative products and services. These include foreign-exchange and derivative products and risk management, corporate finance, and investment management. However, Singapore government's reluctance to internationalize the local dollar has so far effectively prevented the launch of any futures instruments based on the local economy or denominated in Singapore dollars. Political sensitivity makes it difficult for Simex to launch products based on the markets of close neighbors such as Malaysia, Indonesia, and Thailand.

While Simex looks for new ways to expand, there are signs that derivatives are gaining acceptance in other Southeast Asian nations. Malaysia is the pioneer of a different model from Singapore; it is creating a derivatives-market denominated in its domestic currency and based on local instruments. Indonesia and Thailand are observing developments with interest. Malaysia's asset is its stock market, the third largest in Asia after Tokyo and Hong Kong. In late 1995, it launched the Kuala Lumpur options and Financial Futures Exchange (Kloffe) offering the first stock index futures contracts in Southeast Asia that are denominated in a local currency. In early 1996, the Malaysian Monetary Exchange (MME) opened to offer the world's first ringgit interest rate futures. There are signs of an over-the-counter market in Kuala Lumpur in interest rate swaps between local banks and corporate customers. By trading the three-month Klibor (Kuala Lumpur Interbank Offered Rate) contract on the MME, banks are also looking into quoting forward rate agreements for their corporate clients. Driven partly by the requirements of market players to hedge their risk in the recently falling market, average daily turnover rose recently in 1997. Malaysian institutional investors remain slow to use the facilities.

Currency Trading

Asian major currencies are some of the more liquid currencies, such as the Singapore dollar, the Thai baht, the Malaysian ringgit, and the Hong Kong dollar. Other less liquid currencies such as the South Korean won, the Taiwan dollar, the Philippines peso, and the Vietnamese dong are sometimes thought of as Asian minors.

Singapore is the fourth largest currency trading center in the world and the largest center of non-yen trade in Asia. Tokyo surpasses it if yen trade is included. The average daily turnover in 1996 was more than U.S.$190 billion. A total of 220 international and merchant banks keep offices in Singapore of which 80 have made the island their regional headquarters for at least some of their operations.

Many banks are driven to Southeast Asia by overcapacity in the industry in Europe and in the United States and by a general decrease in volatility in G-7 currencies. What is less certain is the extent to which Singapore's emergence has come at the expense of Hong Kong. There are some significant movements in treasury operations from Hong Kong to Singapore over the past two years.

Although some institutions target multinationals, others are increasingly targeting domestic corporate clients by setting up a network of offices across the region. There are also monies to be won and lost by speculating on Asian currencies. The spread between the bid and offer prices of such currencies is often much wider than on their G-7 counter parts. Currently, most Asian currency trading is conducted through the dollar, but yen cross-trading against Asian currencies will increase because of the yen's important role in trade and debt in the region.

The significant level of political and economic uncertainty in several Southeast Asian nations is helping to provide a level of currency volatility. Southeast Asian nations have for years put emphasis on currency stability. They regard it as an essential precondition to attract manufacturing investments needed for economic developments. Consequently, bank treasury operations are often want to be seen as not just speculators, but as providers of a hedging service to corporate clients.

Trade Restrictions on Financial Services

Asian barriers to entry have begun to come down, but overseas investors have been repeatedly frustrated by the failure of countries to follow up on pledges of liberalization. Indonesia is acutely aware that growing levels of foreign investment are essential to its economic development plans, particularly as it faces increasing competition for funds from China, Vietnam, India, and Eastern Europe. Indonesia has promised to remove all restrictions by 2020, but it has yet to produce a plan of action. A decree issued three years ago, allowing 100 percent foreign ownership of companies, has never been carried out, and access to foreign financial service providers remains mostly limited to minority shares in joint ventures.

The Philippines has moved since 1994 from a nearly closed market to one offering a roughly level playing field for foreign banks that have operated in the country. However, newcomers are subject to restrictions, and promises made in the Uruguay Round have not always been matched by domestic legislation. Given the present economic conditions, there is not much political support for further opening the market.

Asia's intentions are crucial to the recent attempts at concluding a multilateral pact on financial services. In 1995, the European Union and other countries have agreed to a partial liberalization on financial services, which kept the issue afloat. The U.S. financial services coalition has broadened with the addition of new securities firms and financial information providers. Whereas the goal in 1995 was for higher equity levels in banks, the new members put greater stress on gaining the right to operate with flexibility. Securities firms increasingly have been following their business clients overseas. However, local laws prevent them from structuring their businesses efficiently, or even establishing offices. They faced investment limits, strict foreign-exchange controls, curbs on the introduction of new products, and complicated, sometimes impenetrable, regulatory barriers.

In Malaysia, progress was slow. The government is highly interventionist, regulatory, and inflexible. Access for foreign companies is severely restricted to minority share holding. It limits access for new companies in all sectors, with a few exceptions, such as charge card companies and offshore banks. New branching operations are not allowed, and the number of foreign managers and specialists allowed to work in Malaysia is restricted. Insurance companies are forced to restructure and divest to a minority foreign share holding.

In Korea, reforms began in financial services after it joined the Organization for Economic Cooperation and Development (OECD). However, there are still many restrictions. Foreign participation in financial services is limited to 15 percent. Foreign ownership is limited to 50 percent of banking joint ventures and 49 percent of life insurance. Foreign banks in Korea face many curbs. Access is limited in the credit card market. Loans from foreign bank branches to single customers are limited to 15 percent of capital for direct loans and 30 percent for indirect liabilities. Banks must obtain government approval for increases in their paid-in capital. Limits are imposed on refinancing, operations in local currency, local financing for foreign companies, and issuing of certificates of deposit.

In Singapore, foreign banks are limited to only one office, unless they were in the country before 1972. Foreign banks are prohibited from opening new subbranches or establishing off-premise automatic teller machines (ATMs). Access to local electronic banking services is heavily restricted. Offshore banks are forbidden to participate in core banking activities and many routine transactions such as dollar loans to nonresidents require government approval.

Thailand is gradually opening its market to foreign institutions. The government refuses licenses to wholly owned subsidiaries. The number of foreign banks entering offshore is limited and new access to the domestic market is confined to foreign banks with offshore licenses. Foreign investment in existing or new Thai banks is capped at 25 percent. Thai authorities have expressed a desire to develop and internationalize their domestic debt market. This is more evident in the relaxation of the restrictions on Thai entities issuing debentures and other debt instruments than in allowing foreign financial institutions to become involved in the domestic market.

India has been taking cautious steps toward liberalization. Foreign banks are limited to a 15 percent share of the banking system's assets, and they pay higher tax rates (48 percent) than do domestic banks (35 percent). Foreign securities firms have helped raise badly needed new capital. It is not yet clear when tax treatment and profit repatriation restrictions will be eased. India has long resisted pressure to liberalize its insurance sector. Foreign providers are limited to cross-border trade in marine and aviation insurance or reinsurance for residual uncovered risk not placed with Indian companies. The government requires remittances from abroad for all expenses incurred by insurance resident representatives.

China's barriers are the steepest in Asia, but until the World Trade Organization deal is finalized, little leverage can be exerted to open up China.

Analysis of Recent Turmoils

The success of Asian countries can be measured by the gap between the output per person in the "tiger" economies and that in the most advanced countries. Asian economies have been trying to narrow these gaps through successful industrial policies and trade policies.

Between 1970 and 1995, the gross national product per head of South Korea went up almost elevenfold, of Hong Kong fourfold, and of Thailand by 3.5-fold. In 1970, Korea's real income per head (at purchasing power parity) was 15 percent of the U.S. level. By 1995, it was more than 40 percent of the U.S. level. Thailand's income per head has risen from 11 to 28 percent of U.S. levels over the same quarter of a century. The instruments used by these countries are prudent industrial policies, high savings rates, removals of obstacles to exports, competitive real exchange rates, appropriate interventions in the market, and mass education. The question is whether these policies are sustainable after the recent turmoils. There is no reason that the world economy will not permit them to do so. Although East Asian economies have to compete with China, China's growth can create more opportunities for them as well. The explanations for the recent turmoils are obvious. They lie in the rise of U.S. dollars against the yen, wrongly managed exchange rates, and immature financial systems. During the weakness of the dollar up to spring 1995, East Asian economies with currencies linked to the dollar enjoyed high levels of competitiveness, particularly against the producers in Japan. That helped these economies to achieve exceptional growth; the Thai economy expanded at an average rate of 8.4 percent a year between 1990 and 1995.

Rapid growth had stimulated large-scale capital inflows. Thailand had a current account deficit of about 7 percent of its GNP between 1990 and 1995 financed by these capital inflows. If there was a floating exchange rate, there should be depreciation of Thai currency. Due to the fixed exchange rates in Thailand, inflationary excess demands were rising stimulated by low interest rates, and that has resulted into high levels of borrowing to support property developments. When the dollar started to appreciate, Thailand's exports began to suffer, due to appreciating Thai currency with the result of diminishing competitiveness (China devalued severely in 1994). There was also an added factor, the declining world demands for electronics. The devaluations of the currencies for all the countries in Southeast Asia can restore their competitiveness against China in particular and have paved the way for future growth. However, all of them have to reduce their budget deficits and devalue their currencies, which in the short run create difficulties.

Along with these difficult situations, a new idea has emerged: an Asian currency support fund supported by Japanese finance. According to Japan, reserves of some U.S.$100 million can be used by Japan to support this fund. Asian countries have small quotas with the IMF and are restricted as to how much they can borrow. A fund that could top up loans from the IMF would be particularly helpful as most Asian countries are already using Japanese finance quite heavily. Japanese banks have serious exposure to the region, and the area is crucial for Japan's exports and foreign direct investments. However, Western countries are bitterly opposed to the idea, as they feel that they will have fewer controls over the affairs of the Asian countries that they exert through the IMF.

Japan and the Asian Economic Crisis

The Asian economic crisis started in the middle of 1997 when a large conglomerate in Korea defaulted and the stock market in Thailand started collapsing along with its currency. Very soon, one country after another was experiencing a combination of massive depreciations of their currencies, sharp downfall of stock prices, a flood of outflows in foreign investments, and bankruptcies of big and small companies. Within a year, the so-called "tiger" economies of East Asia were reduced to begging for economic assistance to survive, with their populations suffering from mass unemployment, social upheavals, and political disturbances not seen in this part of the world for decades. Japan was both a part of the problem and the solution. Japan's own economic recessions since 1991 have contributed to the problem and it is in a position more than any other country or even international financial organization to pave the way for a solution. We discuss here the issue and the actions taken by the Japanese government in some detail.

Sharp depreciation of currencies have caused rise in the prices of imports, increased foreign debt in local currencies for the corporations and banks, and sharp increases in interest rates to prevent capital outflows. The result was a fall in consumption and investments and as a result deep economic downturns. The emergency financial policies adopted in those countries as suggested by the IMF led to contractions of consumption and investments as a result of reductions of public expenditures and money supplies. Financial and credit functions became paralyzed in some countries and the currency crisis became an economic crisis. A high degree of interdependency in both investments and trade formed during the high-speed economic growth caused the East Asian currencies to follow each other down. According to the Asian Development Bank, real economic growth in Southeast Asia in 1998 slowed to –6.9 percent, compared to 8.2 percent in 1995 and 7.1 percent in 1996, due to the effects of the Asian crisis. Inflation in the Southeast Asian region in 1998 was 21.0 percent as compared to 5.6 percent in 1997 and 6.6 percent in 1996.

South Korea, Indonesia, Thailand, and Malaysia had negative growth in 1998.

There are a number of reasons behind the crisis, both long-term and short-term. Inherent structural aspects of the crisis should not be ruled out. In order to maintain a high growth rate, private projects have received government guarantees, subsidies, and public finance. Public industrial and financial policies were geared to enhance corporate profits. Costs and risks of industrial projects were overlooked as the prospects of public "bailout" was the rule for the corporate sector, which was highly connected through political and family ties to the government. It was obvious even in mid-1990s that the profitability of new investments projects was low. In Korea, for example, twenty of the largest thirty conglomerates in 1996 reported negative rates of return on invested capital. In 1997, seven out of the largest thirty conglomerates in Korea were effectively bankrupt (OECD, 1998). However, both the growth of investments and capital flows remained high due to the fall in interest rates in major industrialized countries (interest rates in Japan were almost zero) and the corresponding higher interest rates in Asia. Lax supervision, weak regulations, corrupt practices due to nepotism, semimonopolistic relations between companies and their main banks, and absence of scrutiny from the stock markets due to overdependence of the corporate sector on banks rather than on the stock markets contributed to the growing nonperforming loans. These practices are also common in Japan, and as a result, the Japanese financial system was, until rescued by the government in 1999, buried under the mountain of nonperforming loans. Asian countries have liberalized their capital account of the balance of payments and relaxed restrictions of their financial markets. These have led to significant inflows of foreign institutional funds of a short-term nature, ignoring any possible risks of future defaults due to high economic growth financed by these inflows. This is a classic case of financial "pyramid" building, which can collapse if high economic growth cannot be sustained. By the end of 1996, the share of short-term liabilities in total liabilities was above 50 percent and the ratio of short-term external liabilities to foreign reserves was above 100 percent in Korea, Indonesia, and Thailand.

In the face of negative circumstances, the anticipation of a future bailout has provided international banks strong incentives to take on even more risks. Several Asian countries had experienced serious current account deficits during the 1990s. The current account deficit in Thailand was over 6 percent of GDP for most of the years since 1990 and had reached about 9 percent in 1995 and 1996. Similarly, in Malaysia, the deficit was above 10 percent in 1993, but fell to 3.7 percent in 1996. Indonesia experienced deficits over 4 percent in 1990 and about 3 to 4 percent during 1995–1996. In Korea, deficits were low during the early 1990s (1 to 3 percent of GDP) and had reached 6 percent in 1996. The Philippines had experienced deficits above 5 percent of GDP for a long period during 1990s. These deficits are due largely to trade deficits signifying fall in exports and rise in imports. The exchange rates of these countries, which were tied to the U.S. dollar to provide security to foreign investors, were appropriate only up to 1994–1995. In 1994, when China had devalued its currency by about 50 percent, much of the competitiveness of the Asian countries disappeared. The appreciation of the dollar against the yen since 1995 has also appreciated Asian currencies, however, the rate of appreciation was not that alarming. By taking 1990 as the base year, the real exchange rate had appreciated by 19 percent in Malaysia, 23 percent in the Philippines, 12 percent in Thailand, 8 percent in Indonesia, 18 percent in Singapore, and 30 percent in Hong Kong. In Korea and Taiwan, the currency depreciated in real terms by 14 percent and 10 percent, respectively. However, we have to understand that most of these appreciations took place in 1995.

Fiscal balance, savings rate, and inflation could not pose any serious problems for the region. We can identify some crucial factors responsible for the crisis, which are inefficiency of investments, dependency on foreign loans and short-term capital inflows, China's drive for exports, and Japan's economic recessions (Table 6.1).

High economic growths in Asia had created the impression that current account deficits were sustainable. Growth rates averaging more than 7 percent of GDP was the norm for most countries in the region. The expectations of sustained economic growth had created massive flows of foreign investments and have downplayed the costs of a strategy of excessive dependency on foreign capital. If the boom of investments is restricted to the nontraded sector, investments financed by foreign capital can contribute to the external sector if they can contribute positively to the traded sector. In Asian countries during the 1990s, investments were well above 30 percent of GDP, however, these investments may not have contributed much for real productive activities. In most East Asian countries, construction of luxury houses, hotels, tourist resorts, and golf courses are considered investments, although these can very well be conspicuous consumption, contributing nothing much to the external sector and the country's ability to repay foreign loans. Profitability of investment projects are measured by the Incremental Capital-Output Ratio (ICOR), which is defined as the ratio between the rate of investment and the rate of growth of output. In the Asian region, ICOR increased sharply from 1993 to 1996, thus, the efficiency of investment was falling in the region well before the crisis. In Korea, it was obvious when a number of large conglomerates went bankrupt in 1997. The average debt–equity ratios of thirty large companies was 333 percent (the average for U.S. corporations is about 100 percent). Net

Table 6.1

Gross National Expenditure (Real Terms) and Components: Japan 1995-1998 (% change from year earlier)

	1995	1996	1997	1998
Real GDP	2.8	3.2	–0.7	0.1
Private consumption	3.1	2.8	–1.2	0.9
Residential investment	-6.7	13.7	–21.1	–8.7
Nonresidential investment	7.4	9.1	0.7	–5.1
Government consumption	2.7	1.0	–0.0	0.2
Public investment	7.9	–2.7	–7.2	5.0
Goods and Services Exports	4.6	5.1	9.2	–0.9
Goods and Services Imports	15.2	8.7	–2.9	–5.9

Source: Economic Planning Agency, Japan

profits and returns on invested capital for most large conglomerates (Chaebols) in Korea were very low, too.

If we use conventional criteria, the debt–GDP ratios for most countries in the Asia-Pacific region were low, except for Indonesia (57 percent in 1996), the Philippines (53 percent in 1995), and to some extent in Thailand (33 percent in 1996). The share of short-term debt to total debt was 25 percent in Korea in 1994, 25 percent in Indonesia in 1996, 28 percent in Malaysia in 1996, 70 percent in Thailand, but 19 percent in the Philippines. During the 1990s, the debt service ratio (the interest on all debt plus the principal to be repaid on long-term debt as a share of total exports) was below 10 percent for most countries, except Indonesia (30 percent in 1995), the Philippines (16 percent in 1995), and Thailand (13 percent in 1994 and 11.6 percent in 1995). However, if we look at the solvency factor, a different picture may emerge. The ratio of short-term debt to foreign reserve was 54 percent in 1994 in Korea, 177 percent in Indonesia in 1996, 100 percent in 1996 in Thailand, 79 percent in 1996 in the Philippines, 41 percent in 1996 Malaysia compared with 24 percent in 1996 in China. The ratio of debt service plus short-term debt was 85 percent in 1994 in Korea, 294 percent in 1996 in Indonesia, 69 percent in 1996 in Malaysia, 137 percent in 1996 in the Philippines, 123 percent in 1996 in Thailand compared with 38 percent in 1996 in China. Although China escaped from the crisis, others could not because China's economy was protected from the sudden outflows due to existing restrictions on the capital account of the balance of payments but lender of short-term foreign funds did not have such a leverage on China as they had in other Asian countries affected by the crisis.

The ratio of foreign liabilities to assets reached 1,103 percent in Thailand in 1996, 375 percent in Korea, 424 percent in Indonesia, 172 percent in the Philippines, 165 percent in Hong Kong, 148 percent in Malaysia, and 120 percent in China. In the presence of a rapid currency depreciation, these imbalances may cause serious financial problems if foreign lenders refuse to extend the credit lines to domestic banks. This has happened not only to the Asia-Pacific region in 1997, but also in Brazil and Russia in 1998,

The negative role China has played to contribute to the crisis was downplayed by an IMF analysis (IMF, 1998), perhaps because of political reasons. The development strategy based on exports, supported by open access to U.S. and European markets along with import controls again supported by the Western powers has helped Japan, Korea, Taiwan, and Hong Kong to achieve extraordinary economic growth. This model was adopted in Indonesia, Malaysia, Singapore, Thailand, and to some extent in the Philippines since the mid-1970s and caused high growth. However, it has also caused the development of excess capacity in East Asia, particularly when China decided to join the game in the mid-1980s. China as a latecomer but with very low wages decided to attract foreign investments with the exclusive purpose (at least in the beginning) to export. It used both various export subsidies and exchange-rate devaluations to promote its exports and drive out exports from the ASEAN countries in particular.

Since 1990, China was devaluating its currency, and in 1994, it devalued its currency by about 50 percent, causing tremendous price cuts for Chinese exports. ASEAN countries are unable to cope when they have to maintain a stable currency to attract foreign investments. China was not interested in short-term investments, but the very low wage costs in China and the potential huge domestic market of China were enough incentives for foreign investors. During 1997 and early 1998, when Southeast Asian countries were experiencing difficulty in maintaining exports, Chinese exports were increasing at a fantastic rate. These differences became more acute during 1998. Table 6.2 provides a detailed analysis of how China has destroyed the export markets of some Southeast Asian countries. Exports and imports grew steadily in East Asia until 1995. In 1996, the year before the currency crisis, growth in exports and imports slowed drastically to 4.2 and 4.9 percent, respectively. Both China and the Philippines gained; however, the gain of the Philippines was only marginal. Although competition from China in the Japanese market was limited to a few products, in the U.S. market it is more evident. As a result, labor-intensive exports from Southeast Asia, such as footwear and clothing, have suffered immensely due to Chinese competition (Table 6.2).

The negative part played by Japan in the Asian economic crisis was due to its own failure to recover from the recession that has gripped it since 1991. It had several effects in terms of the reduction of imports from East Asia and the reduction of direct investment flows toward these countries. The Asian crisis also reduced Japanese exports to these countries, which in turn intensified the economic problems in Japan and further reduced its ability to import from East Asia and to provide foreign investments.

Japan has experienced difficulties since 1991, when the Bank of Japan raised the discount rate from 2.5 to 6 percent with the result of a crash in the stock market along with decreasing property and land prices. A banking system that has accepted property, land, and stocks as collateral started experiencing nonperforming loans as a result. From 1992 to 1995, annual economic growth was below 1 percent. The government introduced expansionary fiscal measures but failed to solve the problem of bad loans, which reduced or eliminated the ability of the banking system to continue lending to the corporate sector. Reduction of available credits means companies were unable to expand or to even maintain their operations at the same level, setting off a spiralling recession. The amount of bad debts in 1997 amounted to ¥28.78 trillion. The initial reaction of Japanese companies after the collapse of the bubble economy to avoid recession and falling sales in the home economy was to go abroad. That was the reason for the upsurge of Japanese foreign investments in recent years. However, a prolonged recession in Japan has reduced the funds available for overseas investments, which along with the reduced profitability and economic collapse of the East Asian countries have reduced Japanese foreign investments along with home investments. Table 6.1 gives the picture of the Japanese economy since 1995, showing the declining rate of growth of the GDP, consumption, investments, and imports; the only bright picture was provided by exports.

The Asian crisis had a major impact on Japan when 40 percent of Japan's export went to East Asia and 34 percent of Japan's imports were from East Asia in 1997. Even the United States was not so important for East Asia, whose corresponding figures in 1997 were 18 and 22 percent, respectively. Japan's exports to East Asia was reduced by 22.5 percent in the first half of

Table 6.2

Trade Destructions Caused by China (US$ million)

Categories of goods whose exports to the United States fell by over US$1 million in 1995-1996 and whose exports by China to the United States increased.

Categories of Goods Exported	Decrease in Malaysia	Increase in China
Malaysia		
Skirts, knitted, synthetic fibers	3.130	2.230
Nightshirts,pajamas,of cotton	5.040	43.230
Clothing for infants, synthetic fiber	3.820	4.810
Men's or boys' overcoats, car coats, capes, etc.	2.170	31.960
Women's or girls' overcoats, car-coats, etc.	1.180	11.640
Tin alloys	3.600	7.560
Fittings for looseleaf binders	7.740	22.120
Lamps	1.110	121.160
Thailand		
Frozen fish	5.180	22.890
Silicon dioxide	1.340	7.380
Tubes, pipes, hoses, of plastic	1.980	2.440
Gloves	3.810	13.860
Footwear	2.310	28.780
Soles for footwear	1.790	12.700
Seats, etc.	1.720	19.210

Source: MITI and JETRO

1998 compared to the same period in 1997. Imports for the same period fell by 17.7 percent. However, before the Asian crisis in 1996, Japan's exports to ASEAN countries fell by 4.4 percent and imports rose by 9 percent. During the period of January to March 1998, the most severe months for the crisis, the United States trade deficit with the ASEAN grew by U.S.$1.2 billion and Japan's trade deficits with the ASEAN grew by U.S.$1.8 billion. Thus, it is questionable to put the blame for the crisis on the fall of Japan's imports. It is certainly true though that due to the recessions at home, Japan was unable to protect East Asia from the crisis (Table 6.3 and Figure 6.1).

Japan's exports during 1998 were reduced by 11 percent to Thailand, 21.2 percent to Malaysia, 38.2 percent to Indonesia, and 20.8 percent to Singapore, whereas exports rose by 15.4 percent to China, and by 9.4 percent to South Korea. Japan's imports declined by 15.4 percent from Thailand, 18.6 percent from South Korea, 22.8 percent from Malaysia, 29.6 percent from Indonesia, 20.3 percent from China, and 17.7 percent from Singapore.

Table 6.3

Trade Activities of Japanese Manufacturers, 1996 (U.S.$ million, %)

	Japanese share of imports	Exports	Exports by Japanese firms	Japanese share of exports	Imports	Imports by Japanese firms
Thailand	55,789	25,091	45.0	73,484	11,079	15.1
Indonesia	48,059	11,157	23.2	42,945	6,586	15.3
Malaysia	78,246	14,884	19.0	77,797	10,520	13.5
Phillippines	20,543	5,604	27.3	31,756	3,686	11.6

Source: MITI

Figure 6.1 **Japanese Firms' Share of Exports from ASEAN4 by Destinations, 1996**

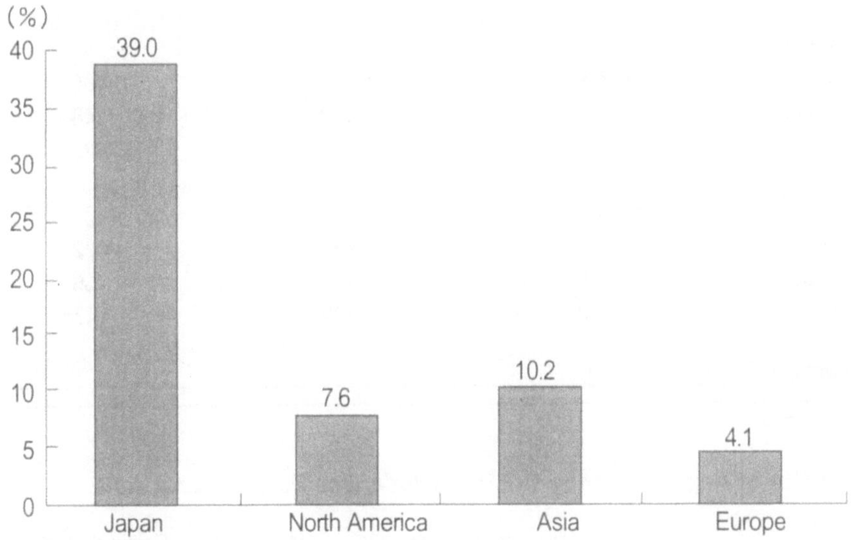

Source: JETRO

Japanese foreign investments fell by 48 percent in four major ASEAN countries (Indonesia, Thailand, Malaysia, and the Philippines), 14 percent in China, and 50 percent in Hong Kong from mid-1997 to mid-1998. During the same period, investments rose by 1.8 percent in South Korea, Taiwan, Hong Kong, and Singapore, although these investments do not reflect expansion of productive capacities of Japanese companies but expansion of equity bases of Japanese partners in joint-venture

Table 6.4

FDI Inflows to ASEAN4 (based on approved investments, US$ million, %)

Source	1996	1997	Ist half of 1998
Thailand			
Total	13,124	11,784	2,945
Japan	6,191	5,021	801
U.S.	2,766	1,785	44
Indonesia			
Total	29,931.4	33,833	8,344
Japan	7,655.3	5,421	898
U.S.	642.1	1,018	272
Malaysia			
Total	6,779	4,101	1,450
Japan	1,150	818	348
U.S.	1,831	886	639
Philippines			
Total	967	1,940	672
Japan	58	136	56
U.S.	33	182	147

Source: JETRO

Table 6.5

Impacts of Asian Currency Crisis on Japanese Firms in East Asia

	Fall in sales due to fall in local demand	Increase in cost of procurement of imported parts	Increase cost of interest payments	Fall in exports
Total percentage of firms that responded	64.7	57.4	30.2	19.1
Textiles	22.2	33.3	33.3	22.2
Electric machinery	65.6	59.4	28.1	18.8
Motor vehicles	92.1	60.5	36.8	60.5

Source: JETRO

Table 6.6

Impacts of Asian Crisis on Operations of Japanese Firms in East Asia

	Reduction in operating ratio	Rise in operating ratio	Restructuring through layoffs	Raised local procurements	Shifts from local sales to exports
Textiles	0.0	44.4	11.1	11.1	44.4
Electric machinery	40.6	15.6	31.3	31.3	18.8
Motor vehicles	63.2	7.9	50.0	10.5	21.1

Source: JETRO

operations taking advantage of the low costs of shares. Japanese foreign investments were falling, since 1996 investments in the textile industry in China and investment in machinery in East Asia fell significantly (Table 6.4).

The fall in Japanese investments in East Asia was due to the problems Japanese companies have faced since the crisis fell on them. According to a survey conducted by JETRO (Japan External Trade Organization), 92 percent of the automobile companies, 65 percent of the electrical machinery companies, and 64 percent of all Japanese companies in 1998 have experienced a fall in sales of local demand. Sixty percent of the automobile companies have also experienced increased costs of procurements and a fall in exports (Tables 6.5 and 6.6).

As a result, Japanese automobile giants are reducing their operations and laying off workers. Similarly, 30 percent of the textile and electrical machinery industries of Japanese origin are reducing their operations. They are also shifting from the domestic to the export market to avoid the depressing pictures of the host countries.

Table 6.7 shows the decline of Japanese investments during the crisis period in four major ASEAN countries. For all four countries, Japanese investments, which are in the form of direct investments, declined. At the same time, U.S. investments, which are mainly in the form of equity investments through mergers and acquisitions, fell in Thailand and Malaysia but increased in Indonesia and in the Philippines.

The Japanese government could not ignore the crisis in East Asia. It has recently taken a series of measures to solve its own economic problems and to help the countries in East Asia. The package of the financial and trade support to East Asia in 1998 has reached U.S.$30 billion of which U.S.$15 billion was available for medium- to longer-term finan-

Table 6.7

Export Growth Rates in East Asian Economies (%)

	1997												1998			
	1	2	3	4	5	6	7	8	9	10	11	12	1	2	3	4
South Korea	–9.0	–5.3	–3.1	7.1	4.5	9.6	19.3	14.0	13.4	5.2	3.8	1.7	–0.3	19.9	6.6	6.6
Thailand	3.1	–7.6	2.3	2.2	–1.5	–5.1	5.8	0.7	9.9	10.7	–0.5	–1.4	–11.8	–4.9	–10.5	
Malaysia	6.6	6.3	5.5	–1.6	1.1	1.2	4.5	2.5	0.9	–2.6	–2.4	–11.0	–23.2	8.9	–12.9	
Indonesia	17.8	10.7	3.3	3.7	11.8	6.8	12.7	8.8	8.7	1.9	5.0	0.5	–2.2	–6.5	11.5	
China	27.6	13.8	35.0	30.0	25.0	25.3	25.1	13.4	23.4	17.1	23.0	4.7	8.4	23.5	9.5	

Source: JETRO

cial need. Another U.S.$15 billion was available for short-term needs to provide adequate liquidity to these affected countries. We have to remember that the total support of the IMF was about U.S.$13 billion. In addition, Japan's Export-Import Bank would provide guarantees on international bank loans, sovereign bonds, and export credits to East Asian countries. Japan also has established an Asian Currency Crisis Support Facility that will provide interest subsidies to allow borrowers to raise funds at a smaller cost. Japan suggested in 1996, before the crisis had emerged, the establishment of an Asian Monetary Fund separate from the control of the International Monetary Fund. However, due to the objections raised by the U.S. government, it did not materialize. The IMF responded to the Asian crisis by contracting credit further through restricted monetary and fiscal policies while these countries were suffering from a liquidity crisis due to the fall of their export revenues and outflows of foreign capital.

Total Japanese bank lending to East Asia in 1998 was about U.S.$274 billion. Thus, the solution of the Japanese banking crisis will not only stimulate the Japanese economy, but will also provide increasing liquidity to the crisis-affected countries. The Japanese government has started nationalizing banks in Japan that are on the verge of bankruptcy and providing public funds to all banks that need it so as to protect them from collapsing. These along with fiscal expansion and the reduction of personal and corporate tax rates will stimulate the economy by providing adequate capital base to the banks, which in turn will help them to provide new investment funds for the corporate sector. Any upturn of the Japanese economy will have a significant positive impact on the economy of East Asia.

7

STRATEGIC MANAGEMENT OF JAPANESE MULTINATIONALS

Japanese manufacturing organizations have made a lot of inroads in overseas production bases. The successes of their enterprises have raised interests on the system of production and organization peculiar to Japanese business firms (Suzaki, 1987; Wickens, 1987). This is particularly true about the automobile production sector where non-Japanese firms are adopting Japanese methods of management in a number of countries in order to compete effectively against Japanese firms (Hayes, 1981; Imai, 1986; Lillrank and Kano, 1989; Monden, 1983; Womack, Jones, and Rees, 1990). The spread of this system is basically due to the foreign production bases of some of the leading Japanese automobile companies. In order to understand the strategic management issues regarding Japanese overseas affiliates, we discuss here the essential characteristics of the Japanese system of management (Hayes, 1981; Shingo, 1981, 1985).

The Japanese system of management is a complete philosophy of organization that can affect every part of the enterprise. There are three basic parts: lean production system, total quality management, and human resources management (Nohara, 1985; Ohno, 1978). These three parts are interlinked in order to produce the total effect on the management of Japanese enterprises. Because Japanese overseas affiliates are part of the parent company, their strategic management is part of the management strategy of the parent company (Abo, 1994; Morita, 1992; Shimada, 1993).

Lean Production System

The basic idea of the lean production system is described in Table 7.1. The fundamental principles are described at the bottom of the table.

Table 7.1

Lean Production System

Lean Production				
Lean Development	+ Lean Procurement	+Lean Manufacturing	+ Lean Distribution	+ Lean Enterprise
Supplier involvement		*Elimination of waste*	*Lean buffers*	*Global network*
Cross functional teams	*Supplier hierarchies*	*Continuous improvement*	*Customer involvement*	*Knowledge structures*
Simultaneous engineering	*Larger subsystems from suppliers teams*	*Multifunctional teams*	*Aggressive marketing*	
Integration instead of coordination	***Zero Defects / JIT***			
Strategic management	*Vertical information systems*			
Black box engineering	*Decentralized responsibilities/ integrated push functions*			
	Pull instead of push			

Fundamental Principles
Multifunctional teams
Vertical information systems
No buffers
No indirect resources
Networks

Source: Toyota Corporation

At all levels, the fundamental idea is "human-ware" (Shimada, 1993), which is described in Figure 7.1. "Human-ware" is defined as the integration and interdependence of machinery and humans and a concept to differentiate between different types of production systems (Shimada, 1993).

Figure 7.1 **Japanese Human-Ware Model**

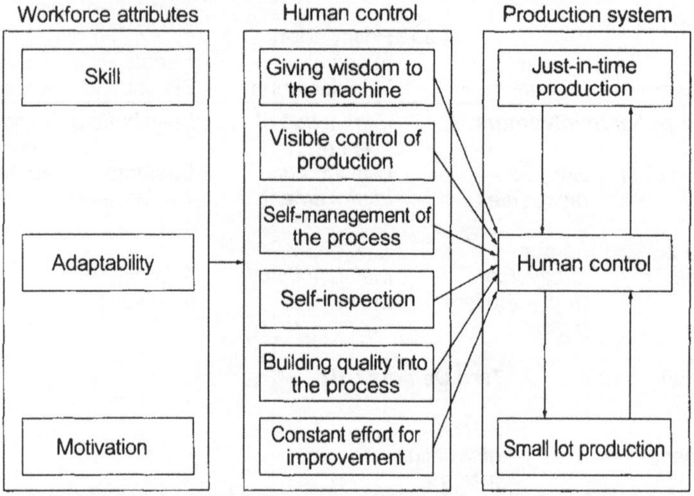

Source: Toyota Corporation

Elimination of Waste

The purpose of the lean production philosophy, which was developed at the Toyota Motor Company, is to lower costs. This is done through the elimination of waste—everything that does not add value to the product. The most important source of waste in the production process is inventory. Keeping parts and products in stock does not add value to them and should be eliminated. In manufacturing, inventory in the form of work in progress is especially wasteful and should be reduced. Apart from being wasteful in itself, inventory also hides other problems. The effects of reducing work in progress go beyond that of reducing capital employed. The reasons for the existence of inventory must be removed. One important way of doing this is by minimizing downtime in machines. This is accomplished through preventive maintenance.

Another way to reduce inventories is through reducing lot sizes. A reduction of lot sizes also has other positive effects such as increasing flexibility since it is possible to switch between different parts more often. However, given that lot sizes are reduced, setup times also have to be reduced.

At Toyota, through an ingenious method (SMED) developed by Shingo (1981, 1985), setup times in large punch presses could be reduced from several hours to less than ten minutes. This had dramatic consequences on lot sizes.

Another source of waste is the transportation of parts. Transporting parts from one location in the factory to another does not add any value to the product. It also adds to manufacturing lead time. If machines can be grouped together in a cell-based layout, the physical connection of the flow of products renders a faster truck useless.

Lack of quality is another source of waste. Manufacturing parts and products that are defective and therefore need to be reworked is wasteful. Even worse is the scrapping of parts. Therefore, eliminating scrap and rework is essential to reduce waste. Manufacturing parts that are fault-free from the beginning have profound consequences for productivity (Flynn, Schroeder, and Sakakibara, 1994).

Continuous Improvement

The constant strive for perfection (*kaizen* in Japanese) is the overriding concept behind good management, in which the production system is being constantly improved; perfection is the only goal. Involving everyone in the work of improvement is often accomplished through quality circles. These are activities in which operators gather in groups to come up with suggestions on possible improvements. There are schemes for implementing suggestions, rewarding employees, and feeding back information on the status of the suggestions.

Zero Defects

In order to attain high productivity, it is essential that all parts and products are fault-free from the very beginning. The goal is to work with products that are fault-free through continuous improvements of the manufacturing system. Thus, zero defects denote how a lean company works in order to attain quality. In a lean production system, it is important to move toward a higher degree of process control. Each process is controlled through knowledge gathered about the parameters of the process. Thus, instead of controlling the parts produced, the process is kept under control. The idea is to prevent defects from occurring through discovering errors that can lead to defects (Lillrank and Kano, 1989;

Oakland, 1993). A lean production system uses autonomous defect controls, which are inexpensive means of conducting inspections of all units to ensure zero defects. Quality assurance is the responsibility of everyone. Identification of defective parts is the responsibility of workers, who are allowed to stop the production line when defective parts are found. Responsibility for adjusting the defective parts is delegated to workers. As a consequence, the number of personnel working in the quality control department can be reduced; the size of the adjustment and repair areas can be reduced, too.

Manufacturing tasks are organized into teams. This makes the workers more aware of the need to manufacture only fault-free parts. An important reason for the improved awareness was that the physical contact between manufacturing stages allowed for better communication. Largely through the use of teams, workers found it beneficial to have the responsibility for correction resting with that part of the process where the error has been committed. Through the use of statistical process control, with tests after each process, the company can better control their production processes

Just-in-Time

Accomplishing fault-free parts is a prerequisite to achieving just-in-time deliveries. The principle of just-in-time means that each process should be provided with the right part, in the right quantity, at exactly the right point of time. The ultimate goal is that every process should be provided with one part at a time, exactly when that part is needed. It is possible to have different levels of just-in-time. First, there is the case when parts are moved between different processes in lots. Second, parts are differentiated according to product variants. Third, there is sequential just-in-time, where parts arrive with reference to the individual products on the line. For example, car seats may arrive at the assembly line in the exact order in which they are needed. In general, the higher the level of just-in-time a company can master the better. However, sequential just-in-time is not always needed. It will vary depending on the nature of the products. When the products are standardized and relatively inexpensive, it may not be too important to achieve the highest level of just-in-time.

Pull Instead of Push

Scheduling materials is closely related to the principle of just-in-time. It is useful to look at the relationship between forward scheduling and backward request. Before starting to implement lean production in a company, final assembly is made to customer order. In all other stages of the manufacturing process, productions are according to a forecast. Gradually, the number of manufacturing stages producing according to customer order has to be extended. Thus, somewhere in the material flow is a point where pull meets push. Behind this point, backward requests are used. Ahead of this point, there is forward scheduling. This may create difficulties in stock-outs or too large stocks at this pull-push point. This can be due to the difficulties in making correct forecasts (Karlsson and Ahlstrom, 1996).

Multifunctional Teams

The most important feature of the organizational setup of the lean production system is the extensive use of multifunctional teams, which are groups of workers able to perform many different tasks. The teams are organized along a cell-based production flow system. Due to the rotation of the tasks in a team, the increased flexibility reduces the vulnerability of the production system. The number of job classifications also decreases. Workers have received training to perform a number of different tasks, such as statistical process control, work with quality instruments and computers, set up performances, maintenance, and so on. They also have to be trained in a number of functional areas such as materials management, purchasing, maintenance, and quality control. The company rotates the workers among tasks frequently.

Decentralized Responsibilities

In the lean production system, responsibilities are decentralized. There is no supervisory level in the hierarchy. The multifunctional team is expected to perform supervisory tasks. This is done through the rotation of team leadership among workers. As a result, the number of hierarchical levels in the organization can be reduced. The number of functional areas that are the responsibility of the teams increases. People who are not required as a result of the reductions of requirements for indirect controls normally move to other areas because in the Japanese system the company has no layoff policy (Kumazawa and Yamada, 1989).

Vertical Information System

In a multifunctional setup, it is vital to provide information in time and continuously in the production flow. Information can be of two types:

Figure 7.2 **Essential Elements of the Lean Production System**

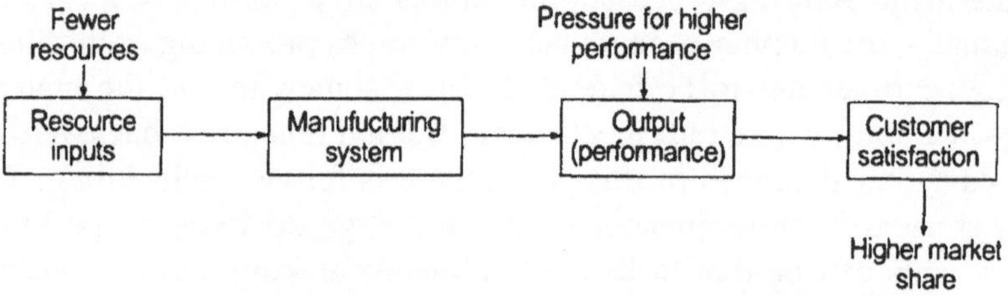

Source: Toyota Corporation

(a) strategic information about the overall performance and plans of the company; and (b) operational information about performance of the teams, quality productivity, lead times, and other factors in the production process. Operational information is more frequent than strategic information about market plans, production plans, process development plans, and financial performance.

Limits to Lean

However, a lean production system is not the only alternative to the traditional production system. There are (a) the German-style quality production model based on a highly skilled work consensus; (b) the systemic rationality model, which is common in information-technology firms; and (c) the Swedish model of the Volvo Motor Company, a reflective production system in which production teams have direct contact with the customers (Altman, 1995; Cusumano, 1994; Jonsson, 1995; Nomura, 1993; Redher, 1994; Sandberg, 1995; Sasaki, 1994). (See Figure 7.2.)

Changes in the Japanese System

Japanese companies no longer depend exclusively on the concept of the lean production system. Due to changes in the external economic environment; collapse of the "bubble economy" of the late 1980s; rise in the exchange value of the yen, which makes Japanese exports too expensive; and rising costs of labor in Japan have provoked changes in the management system of Japanese companies (CJAWU, 1993; Katayama and Bennett, 1996; Miyai, 1995). The main competitive pressure has been to expand market shares. The principal means of achieving that has been through price competition. This in turn has reduced profits, thereby inviting cost reductions and increased revenues. Cost reductions are associated with *kaizen,* continuous improvements, which has stimulated further price competition. Increased revenues need increased sales volumes, new products, and diversified products. That demands new investments, more indirect labor, increasing breakeven point and reductions of profits. During the bubble economy, this continuous cycle was maintained. Now, larger sales volumes are difficult to achieve due to stagnant consumptions. There are also reduced opportunities for Japanese companies to rely on exports as a means of compensating for lower domestic sales.

The production system is changing and gradually adopting a more flexible system with the following characteristics (see Figure 7.3).

(a) The production system is more flexible in order to adapt to changes in demand; this will reduce the cost of production.
(b) The achievements of lower fixed costs using fewer frequent changes in products and fewer replacements of equipment are being achieved.
(c) Technological solutions are being implemented in order to have flexibility in production system design on both downstream and upstream products.
(d) Efforts are there to reduce work-in-progress and setup times by grouping parts and products into families.
(e) Standardized modules of established and reliable design are being incorporated into new products, which allows greater mixing of products.
(f) Mixing of production allows a variety of products to be manufactured without large inventories.
(g) There are extensive usages of *kaizen* activities and TQM (total quality management) and TPM (total productive maintenance).

Strategic Management of Japanese Multinational Companies Overseas

Strategic management of a multinational company involves evaluation of its own domestic competitiveness and utilizing this experience in a global setting. At the same time, the company has to decide the configuration of its operations across the world, that is, where to locate which

Figure 7.3 **Past Trends of Japanese Manufacturing System**

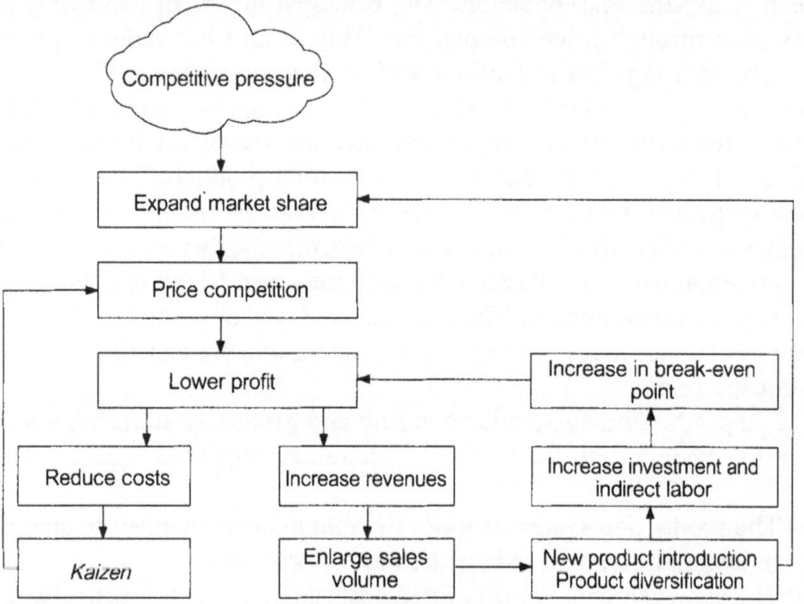

Source: Toyota Corporation

facility. We now present some detailed analysis of two Japanese multinationals, Nissan and Toyota, and examine the basic characteristics of their operations and their style of management.

Nissan

Nissan Motor Manufacturing (UK) Ltd. was established in 1984 as a part of Nissan Japan's global investment strategies. Production started in 1986. In that year, Nissan announced plans to accelerate the UK manufacturing program by increasing local content to 60 percent by 1988 and 80 percent by 1991 with a plan to produce 100,000 units. The local-content element was an obligation to the European Economic Commission; otherwise, the EEC could charge prohibitive tariffs. By 1987, Nissan internalized its sales in the UK, with UK-produced cars becoming the sole source of supply to the UK market. Plans for new investment were made to bring the total investment in the manufacturing plant up to

£610 million. By 1988, 60 percent of the content of the car was made in Europe and the plant was modified to start production of an engine and plastic injection-molding facility. Nissan has also invested heavily in research and development efforts within Europe. Britain was selected by Nissan as its European technology center and a number of affiliated research and development organizations were planned. At the same time, coordination in research and development was enhanced by having design networks between development centers for Nissan in Japan, the United States, and Europe. Exports to European countries started in 1988. In 1991, the production target was raised to 120,000 units. Exports from the UK to East European countries and to Far East Asian countries started that year. In 1992, the production target was raised to 175,000 in response to increased demand in Britain and in Europe. Total investment was raised to £900 million, which was the target Japanese investment in Europe so far. Production of cars was made as self-sufficient as possible, with engines produced in the UK used in all cars produced there. In 1992, further automation of the plant was introduced by installing an automated pressing machine to build the body of the car. In that year, Nissan had its first profit in its UK operation after eight years of investment. With these successes, Nissan enhanced its investment in 1993 by £26 million and a new model was launched. By 1994, Nissan exported cars from its UK production base to thirty-four different world markets. By 1995, Nissan's total investment reached £1.25 billion in the UK and the plant in the UK produced 1 million cars and 1 million engines.

Employment in the UK plant has gone up from 470 in 1986 to 4,038 in 1995. Total production in 1955 reached 215,346 units. Out of that, 161,215 was for export to other countries. Thus, Nissan has successfully used the UK as its export base. At the same time, it has created a network of suppliers throughout Europe. The number of suppliers varies from model to model. This network of suppliers now satisfies most of the needs of production in the UK. The only major components to be imported from Japan for the production of the Primera and Micra are the transmission system and engine block.

The Philosophy of the Company and the Management System in the UK. According to company philosophy, "Nissan's Sunderland (UK) plant aims to build profitably the highest quality car sold in Europe to achieve the maximum possible customer satisfaction and thus ensure the prosperity of the company and its staff." Company's management style reflect this.

Organizational Layout of Production Management System. The Nissan plant in Sunderland, UK, includes a car and component manufacturing facility, an engine machining and assembly plant, a foundry, a plastics injection-and blow-molding plant, and a service parts operation all on one site. Environmental considerations are high on the list of priorities in the production system. The use of water-based paints, increased volume of recycling, and provisions for a good operator environment are some of the priorities. The just-in-time production system is applied throughout internally. Nissan does not build a large buffer stock of doors, bonnets, and boot lids; the total amount of stock in process time in the body assembly plant is less than one hour.

Quality Management. Total quality is a philosophy that runs through every aspect of the business: the way in which the plant is run and the way in which the cars it produces are built. Quality is not something left to the quality control staff. It is the responsibility of every person in the organization. Everyone is fully aware of the valuable and significant role to be fulfilled. Quality of standards and targets are set in all areas and the plant's performance is monitored against these. Results are regularly reviewed and fed back to help improve individual processes. Parts quality is also constantly monitored using special test rigs backed by extensive chemical and metallurgy laboratory facilities. The plant's own quality check process is supplemented at random by Nissan's world auditors.

Human Resources Management System. The aim of the personnel management system in a Nissan plant is to create "mutual trust and cooperation between all people within the plant." It involves teamwork, in which management encourages and values the contribution of individuals who are working together toward a common objective and who continuously seek to improve every aspect of the business. It aims for flexibility in the sense of expanding the role of all staff to the maximum extent possible and puts quality consciousness as the key responsibility above all. The production system builds in quality rather than inspect and rectify. These strict targets are assisted by the fact that the company gives common terms and conditions of employment to all staff. For example, everyone is salaried; there are no time clocks; the sickness benefit scheme, private medical insurance, performance appraisal system, and the canteen are the same for all. The company believes that high-caliber, well-trained and motivated people are the key to success. Training expenditures represent 5.6 percent of total payroll costs. Training time represents 4 percent of staff time.

This emphasis on training has resulted in a sharp increase in productivity; the productivity level of UK workers, which at the beginning of the operation was very low, is now comparable to the productivity level of Nissan in Japan.

In order to examine the characteristics of the supervisory style in Nissan, we have taken the opinions of several people in the plant, both shopfloor workers and higher management. The opinion expressed on the management style can be summarized as follows: The management style is very Japanese in nature. It drives out class distinctions that exist in other industries in the UK, where the managerial staff and workers live separate lives at separate facilities. Equal opportunity for every employee is also a new feature in the UK's industrial management policies. The objectives of partner selection are on the similarities of technology and management practices and on the market entry. Political connection is important, because for a new and a foreign company, it helps to establish smooth relationships in the supply chains and distributions. Major causes for conflict with suppliers are due to different management practices. We have noticed that in Nissan, although there is successful implementation of the internal just-in-time production inventory management system, it is not as successful with external suppliers of components and distributors, who are not yet accustomed to the Japanese system. However, personnel conflict is not an important factor in the problem. The traditional arguments of the economist regarding foreign investment flows are not valid. Exchange control or closeness of raw materials are not important, but developments of new markets, geographical diversification, and future protection of existing markets are important factors along with government's regional policies. These observations are contrary to accepted Western ideas on foreign investment, which demand open foreign trade and no regional policies of the host government.

Impact of Nissan on British Industrial Management. Although it is uncommon that just one foreign company can significantly influence the way the host country runs its industries, something of that nature has taken place in the UK due to Nissan and other Japanese manufacturing companies.

There are three main elements in the improved techniques introduced into UK manufacturing from 1986 to 1996;

(a) A commitment to *kaizen,* or continuous improvement
(b) Cooperative relationships among workers, managers and suppliers
(c) Emphasis on measuring all aspects of business, from serious faults to misplaced labels to identify precisely what needs improvements.

Before the establishments of Japanese manufacturing bases in the UK, UK managers were reluctant to utilize these concepts because of their fear that they might lead to serious industrial disturbances; also, it is not in their psychology to put so much emphasis on nontechnical aspects of manufacturing. With the arrival of Japanese car manufacturing companies such as Nissan, Toyota, and Honda, there has been a compulsion to introduce the Japanese style of management to the UK so as to increase the level of productivity to the Japanese level.

The Japanese effect was introduced through the suppliers of components to Nissan and other Japanese companies. Leading engineering firms like GKN or small companies like Frederick Woolley of Birmingham accepted the standard of quality of these products and the maintenance of the supply line as part of their business deal with Nissan. Even competitors like the Ford Motor Company were forced to change in order to be competitive with the Japanese car manufacturers.

Ford has introduced a Japanese system of a production-inventory system in collaboration with Mazda, another Japanese car market, in their UK plants. The most significant change took place in the Rover car plants, which were in collaboration with Honda of Japan. Honda introduced both the Japanese management system and automated production system to Rover.

However, what is true for the big rival UK car manufacturers is not true for the smaller suppliers of components. The UK has achieved significant improvements in productivity and quality standards, but the supply-chain networks to the large manufacturers are yet to accept fully the Japanese system. Nissan estimates that the number of suppliers meeting its top standard of 10 faults per million parts delivered has risen from 16 out of 200 to about 50 in the past four years ending in 1996. However, the same figure for Japan is about 150.

The Japanese effect weakens with distance from the source. Nissan has influenced small component suppliers such as Frederick Woolley, which supplies to Lucas, which in turn supplies to Nissan. Lucas has influenced its own suppliers. However, Frederick Woolley has less than 100 faults per million parts; its own suppliers score 3,500 or more. The smaller companies farther down the supply chain have little direct contact with the Japanese inspired method.

Some of the larger companies in the UK are having difficulty in accepting Japanese standards. Under Nissan's QCDDM supplier-evaluation system, suppliers are rated for quality, cost, delivery, development of new products and management. Most suppliers accept the first four, but do not like being rated on management.

Nissan's influence is not limited to the motor industry. Managers from all over the UK come to the Nissan plant. The government has sponsored teams of experts to learn from Nissan, Toyota, and Honda. The significant efforts of Japanese investment on UK industrial management are in the drive for quality and a better relationship between managers and the workforce.

Relationship with Nissan's Global Strategy. Nissan's European operations are part of the company's global strategy to diversify production bases. This strategy has two main purposes: (a) to avoid tariff and nontariff restrictions on exports from its Japanese base; (b) to maintain costs by taking into account regional characteristics; (c) to compete effectively with its Japanese rivals at home by producing cars inexpensively abroad and to compete with other foreign manufacturers. Nissan has a tripolar operating structure based in Japan and Asia, the United States and Europe with research and development, and production, sales, and finance capabilities in each region. To further localize overseas production and make it more self-sufficient, the company continues to strengthen sales and local production in each region. At the same time, Nissan is increasing Japan-bound exports from overseas production bases and pursuing a natural supply of components and vehicles on a global level. Other key initiatives are improving cost-competitiveness and constantly raising its own ability to compete on the basis of quality. Nissan is also a strengthening presence in the growth markets of Asia.

Although Nissan performed favorably in the U.S. market, Mexico's distressed economy and increasingly severe price competition in Europe made the operating environment in 1995-1996 outside Japan challenging. Although Nissan's loss is declining in Japan, it is losing continuously because of Japan's recessions. Nissan's goals for the future include expansion of global automobile and component manufacturing capabilities and increasing purchases from cost-competitive overseas parts suppliers. This effort will entail further progress in importing autos made by Nissan plants overseas to Japan. These moves complement efforts to enhance the product lineup, optimize efficiency, and help insulate Nissan against external factors such as currency fluctuation. Nissan's Global Restructuring Policy includes expansion of local vehicle production and local production of major components. Another feature is exports from its overseas production bases. For example, the Terranoll (Mistral) model is now going to Japan from Nissan, South Africa. Nissan, UK, is exporting the Micra (March) model to Australia, and Nissan, Mexico, is exporting the Sentra (Sunny) to the United States.

Stronger overseas R&D functions and parts procurement systems are other parts of the policy. Nissan is planning to increase its R&D base in Asia in order to have a network of design centers connected to each other in Asia, Europe, and North America. This will strengthen its ability to design locally procured components, as well as tailor the vehicles to specific market needs.

Nissan has created the in-house Imports Production Committee whose mission is to increase imports to Japan of both original equipment parts and after-market replacement parts from competitive suppliers. These efforts will continue in the future. Nissan is building an engine and automatic transmission plant in Tennessee and pursuing expansion in local production through joint ventures in China, Thailand, the Philippines, and Indonesia. Although Japanese production has declined, along with Mexico, but in the UK, the United States, Spain, and Asia, production is increasing. Wagons and pickup trucks, designed for the Southeast Asia markets and manufactured in Thailand, Taiwan, the Philippines, and Malaysia, are core models in Nissan's Asian lineup. Nissan plans to double the automobile production in ASEAN countries in cooperation with partners and joint ventures. In Korea, Nissan established its Korean office in Seoul as part of the comprehensive technical assistance agreement with Samsung Motors Inc. This agreement covers development of a new car model for Samsung and support for its other activities. Nissan is also collaborating with Nanking Auto Works (now Yuejin Auto Mobile Group Corp.) in China.

At the same time, Nissan manufactures commercial vehicles in a joint venture with Zengzhou Light Truck Factory in China. Nissan constructed a 12,000-unit-capacity knockdown plant in Indonesia that began production in 1996.

Table 7.2

Training Facilities in Nissan, UK, 1995

Off-the-job training days provided for full-time employees	26,360
Average off-the-job-training days per employee	6.41
Training days provided for trainees	
Average off-the-job training days per trainee	65.84
On-the-job training days provided in production-areas	8,509
Average-on-the-job training days for production staff	3.70
Total number of training days	38,095
Total training expenditure during 1995	£554,8843

Source: NISSAN

Toyota

Toyota was established in Japan in 1937 and its first overseas production began in 1959 in Brazil. Expansion continued throughout the 1950s and 1970s with the spending of several overseas plants in Africa, South America, Southeast Asia, and Australia. In 1985, a joint-venture company was established in the United States, and its own vehicle plants were established in the United States and Canada (in 1988). Toyota (UK) was established in 1989. Production in the UK plant started in 1992; current production is 100,000 units with an investment of £700 million. The engine plant has an investment of £140 million with the current production of 100,000 engine units. The target production capacity was recently raised to 200,000 vehicles with a further investment of £200 million. It is a relatively new plant. Table 7.2 explains the reasons why Toyota has selected the UK as its major production base in Europe.

Production and Operation System. Toyota UK's aim is to satisfy the customer by providing the highest quality at the lowest possible cost in a timely manner with the shortest possible lead time. It has a complete manufacturing operation, including press and weld, paint, plastics, assembly, and engine plus a comprehensive environmental control facility. Quality is built in at every stage and confirmed throughout the process. In the press and welding section, coils of steel are rolled out into "blanks," flat sheets shaped into the basic part in a pattern that minimizes waste steel. Operating to just-in-time production, blanks are cut as required by the press lines. When the press lines require parts to be sent forward, details of orders are entered on computers to ensure timely transfer by automatic guidance vehicle (AGV) to the press machines, the largest of which is capable of exerting a pressure of 4,000 tons. The presses give each part its third dimension using dies. Dies can be changed very quickly so stocks are kept to a minimum according to the Toyota Production System, saving time, money, and space. We have to remember that the so-called Japanese-style production-inventory system, which includes just-in-time production, the *kanban* system, total quality management, cell-based layout designs, was invented in Toyota plants in Japan during the early 1950s.

The completed body panels are welded together (90 percent done by robots) into larger main subassemblies. These subassemblies are then brought together by robots to form a complete body shell. Throughout the process, team members and technology work together to build a high-quality vehicle. At each stage, team members check the quality of the work before passing on the vehicle while a number of automated intelligent systems interact to instruct and control the car-building system. The car then goes through painting, plastic molding of instrument panels, and engine assembly. Despite about 2,500 parts having to be used in each car, there are only two temporary parts storage areas where a maximum of eight hours stock is held. A manifest (printed document) is fixed to the car, containing details of its specifications and providing visual control throughout the assembly process. The car then travels down the assembly line.

Throughout the process, each member is responsible for the quality of work produced and passed on, so a cord along the line enables each member to stop the production line if there is a concern. The cord is pulled once to call support from the team leader; in many cases, the problem is addressed quickly, the cord is pulled again by the team leader, and the line continues never having stopped. If the problem is a little more serious, the team leader will allow the line to stop until the concern is resolved. Although quality is built in at every stage, a complete functional and visual inspection is carried out before the end of the line to ensure complete customer satisfaction.

Management Style. At every level, there are Japanese managers shadowing their local counterparts. This is different from that in Nissan:

These local people are all in command and Japanese managers are very few. There are no local partners for Toyota, unlike Nissan. There are internal just-in-time production and inventory systems, but an external *kanban* system with the supplier is not yet developed. This is because suppliers in Europe have not yet integrated their production and management systems to that of Toyota. In the case of internal management, the style is very similar to that of Nissan, with unified facilities and the same job status for all. Management styles in Toyota are not different from those of Nissan.

Toyota, UK, strives to achieve an organization in which all employees can develop to their full potential. Teamwork is an essential element of Toyota's spending philosophy believing that a well-coordinated group can accomplish far more than the sum of individual efforts. The average age of the workers is only 31; training facilities are built in with the production system. About 100,000 man-days are spent on training prior to production startup. Training is held in all locations throughout the world. UK workers can go for training in Japan, the United States, and Canada, and the workers from Toyota's foreign and Japanese establishments can come to the UK for training. Since the start of production, an additional 20,000 man-days have been spent on specific training courses off the job. The costs and time spent on continuous-on-the job training are almost immeasurable.

Operations and Strategy. In 1995, Toyota, UK, announced expansion plans to achieve a target production capacity of 200,000 vehicles and engines per year. That implied an additional investment of £700 million in vehicle manufacturing and £140 million in engine manufacturing. The production level in 1995 for vehicles was 110,000 per year, and for the engine, 100,000 per year. Currently, Toyota, UK, exports 75 percent of its vehicle production to Europe and the rest is for the UK market. Engines produced by its UK plants are for export as well. In 1999, 15,000 units per year were exported to Turkey; similarly, cylinder blocks and crank shafts were exported to Toyota, Japan. Regarding the supply chain, there are 160 suppliers in ten countries in Europe for parts and components and 50 suppliers in various countries for raw materials. Eighty percent of the supply comes from the UK; there are 80 suppliers of parts and components and 30 suppliers of raw materials from the UK. The amount spent on parts and raw materials are £400 million annually. The main objective of the supply-chain network is to ensure quality. Toyota, UK, is developing long-term partnerships with suppliers based on mutual trust. It has established technical support teams to offer advice and assistance to suppliers on improving quality and efficiency.

Global Strategy. The global strategy of Toyota is to design products for local needs and to produce locally. By 1998, the plan was that Toyota should have the yearly local production capacity for (a) more than one million vehicles in North America; (b) 500,000 vehicles in Asia excluding Japan; (c) and 200,000 vehicles in Europe (i.e., in the UK).

In 1995, plants outside Japan are manufacturing 58 percent of the vehicles Toyota sold that year. The target was to bring that percentage to 65 percent in 1998.

For Toyota, the sales effort is the instrument for globalization of production.

Toyota had started exporting in the 1950s, initially to Southeast Asia and Latin America, and later to North America and Europe. There is now a sales network of 6,600 dealerships in 160 countries throughout the world.

Production followed sales, with Toyota opening its first plants in Latin America in the 1950s and in Asia in the 1960s. These plants were small, producing a few thousand vehicles every year. However, that helped Toyota to avoid paying prohibiting tariffs and to obtain a foothold in the local market. Thus, it was the protectionist policies of those countries that was responsible for local production of Toyotas. Similarly, in order to obtain a presence in a highly protected market, plants were opened in the UK, the United States, and Canada. Design and development became international in the 1970s, when design and technical facilities were set up in North America and Europe. North American plants now manufacture about 900,000 vehicles and that figure reached 1.2 million in 1998. North American operations are localized in the sense that production and management are self-sufficient. Exports from North American operations have reached 66,000 units in 1995.

The operation in Europe is also increasingly localized. The capacity of the engine and vehicle plants in the UK will be expanded by added investments. These plants are exporting to other countries in Europe and throughout the world.

East and Southeast Asia will account for most of the growth in global demand for vehicles. Toyota has opened a second vehicle plant in Thailand in 1996, which has increased the production capacity to 240,000 vehicle per year from 1998. Already, the plants in Thailand have produced one million Toyotas. There is now another plant for Toyota in the Philippines as well, which has raised the production capacity to 60,000 vehicles per year in 1998. In Indonesia, Toyota started production in 1996. In China, there is now a joint-venture company with the Tianjin Automobile Industrial Group to manufacture engines. It supplies engines to an affiliated company, Daihatsu Motor Co., to produce vehicles. In 1996, the Toyota Technical Center in Tianjin was opened to provide technical assistance to local parts manufacturers. In Taiwan, an affiliate company, Kuozui Motors, began production in 1995 and it is now expanding in association with Toyota affiliate Hino Motors of Japan. In Australia, Toyota is producing since 1994 and exporting from there to the Middle East, New Zealand, and other countries of Oceania, with a production capacity of 100,000 units.

After some slowdowns of business, Toyota, Japan, has started its recovery in 1995. However, now its overseas operations are gaining more and more importance. Aggregate business outside Japan accounted for 45.2 percent of net sales in 1995 compared to 40.7 percent in 1994. Thus, soon Toyota will be a global company. Toyota's progress in expanding production capacity outside Japan positions it to serve its principal markets efficiently and cost-effectively with locally made products, which increases its global profits.

Conclusion

Currently, when the yen has depreciated to levels somewhat below its recent peak, prospective economic trends in the United States and Europe are uncertain. The environment for exports from Japan remain severe. Japan is yet to recover from its recessions since 1991, although a gradual recovery is expected. However, a large increase in domestic demand for all these producers discussed are hard to predict. Thus, competition for market share will intensify in the future. Against this background, Japanese automobile companies are maintaining their efforts to enhance competitiveness of their products by bolstering R&D, augmenting efficiency of their manufacturing system, strengthening their sales activities, and further localizing their overseas operations.

CONCLUSION

The analysis has told the story of Japanese foreign investments. The implications of large balance-of-payments surplus of Japan for international capital flows are discussed. The role of Japan in recent Asian economic developments and the implications of Japanese foreign investments on the domestic economy of Japan are analyzed. However, recent turmoils in the Asian economy along with continuous economic recessions in Japan have their consequences for international capital flows.

Japan is also going to have some extensive financial reforms. Given these changing scenarios, what is the future direction of Japanese foreign investments? We think Japan will consolidate its investments in Asia, making investments in proven sectors in safe countries. At the same time, due to its massive involvements in Asian economies, Japan will support a move toward the economic revival of Asian countries. However, in the short term, it is possible that Japanese investment will be attracted more toward Latin America, North America, and Europe. Given the demands of the major economic partners of Japan for deregulation and liberalization of Japan's domestic economy, it is expected that Japan will be involved more closely in global economic affairs.

BIBLIOGRAPHY

Abo, T., ed. (1994). *Hybrid Factory: The Japanese Production System in the United States*. New York: Oxford University Press.

Akamatsu, K. (1961). "A Theory of Unbalanced Growth in the World Economy," *Weltwirtschaftliches Archiv* 86: 196-217.

Aliber, R.Z. (1970). "A Theory of Direct Foreign Investment." In *The International Corporation,* edited by C.P. Kindleberger. Cambridge, MA: The MIT Press.

Altmann, N. (1995). "Japanese Work Policy: Opportunity, Challenge or Threat." In *Enriching Production: Perspectives on Volvo's Uddevalla Plant as an Alternative to Lean Production,* edited by A. Sandberg, pp. 367-381. Aldershot, UK: Avebury.

Baran, P.A, and P.M. Sweezy. (1966). *Monopoly Capital: An Essay on the American Economic and Social Order.* Harmondsworth: Penguin.

Buckley, P., and M. Casson. (1985). *The Economic Theory of the Multinational Enterprise.* London: Macmillan.

Bukharin, N. (1917). *Imperialism and World Economy.* London: Merlin Press.

Cardoso, F.H., and E. Faletto. (1979). *Dependencia y Desarrollo en Americana* Latina. Santiago: Siglo Veintiuno Editors.

Casson, M. (1981). *The Firm and the Market.* Oxford: Basil Blackwell.

Caves, R. (1980). "Investment and Location Policies of Multinational Companies." *Schweiz Zeitschrift fur Volkwirtschaft und Statistik* 116: 321-327.

CJAWU (Confederation of Japan Automobile Workers' Unions). (1993). *Japanese Automobile Industry in the Future.* Tokyo: JAW.

Cowling, K., and R. Sugden. (1987). *Transnational Monopoly Capitalism.* Brighton, UK: Wheatsheaf.

Cusumano, M.A. (1994). "The Limits of 'Lean,'" *Sloan Management Review* (Summer): 27-32.

Dunning, J.H. (1972). *International Investment.* London: Penguin.

———. (1989). "The Theory of International Production." In *International Trade,* edited by K. Fatemi. New York: Taylor and Francis.

———. *Multinational Enterprises and the Global Economy.* Reading, MA: Addison-Wesley.

Ellegard, K., T. Engstrom, B. Johansson, L. Nilsson, and L. Medbo. (1992). *Reflektiv Produktion-Industriell Verksamhet I Forandring. Gothenburg,* Sweden: AB Volvo.

Evans, P. (1979). *Dependent Development: The Alliance of Multinational, State, and Local Capital in Brazil.* Princeton: Princeton University Press.

Flynn, B.B., R.G. Schroeder, and S. Sakakibara. (1994). "A Framework for Quality Management Research and Associated Measurement Instrument." *Journal of Operations Management* 11(4): 339-366.

Ghosal, S. (1987). "Global Strategy: An Organizing Framework," *Strategic Management Review* 8: 425-440.

Hamel, G., and C.K. Prahalad. (1987). "Creating Global Strategic Capability." In *Strategies in Global Competition,* edited by N. Hood and J.E. Vahlne. London: Routledge.

Hayes, R.H. (1981). "Why Japanese Factories Work," *Harvard Business Review* (July–August): 57-66.

Heckscher, E. (1950). "The Effect of Foreign Trade on the Distribution of Income." In *Readings in the Theory of International Trade,* edited by H. Ellis and L.A. Metzler, pp. 272-300. London: Allen & Unwin.

Hobson, J.A. (1907). *Imperialism: A Study.* London: Unwin-Hyman.

Hufbauer, G.C. (1966). *Synthetic Materials and the Theory of International Trade.* London: Duckworth.

Hymer, S.H. (1960). *The International Operations of National Firms: A Study of Direct Foreign Investment.* Cambridge, MA: The MIT Press.

———. (1970). "The Efficiency (Contradictions) of Multinational Corporations," *American Economic Review* 160 (2): 441-448.

Imai, M. (1986). *Kaizen, The Key to Japan's Competitive Success.* New York: McGraw-Hill.

International Monetary Fund. (1988). *Growth in East Asia.* Washington, DC: IMF.

Jonsson. D. (1995). "Lean Production in the Automobile Industry: Second Thoughts." In *Enriching Production: Perspectives on Volvo's Uddevalla Plant as an Alternative to Lean Production,* edited by A. Sandberg, pp. 367-381. Aldershot, UK: Avebury.

Karlsson, C., and P. Ahlstrom. (1996). "Assessing Changes Towards Lean Production," *International Journal of Operations & Production Management* 116 (2): 25-39.

Katayama, H., and D. Bennet. (1996): "Lean Production in a Changing World: A Japanese Perspective," *International Journal of Operations & Production Management* 116 (2): 8-23.

Kenen, P.B. (1994). *The International Economy.* Cambridge: Cambridge University Press.

Kindleberger, C.P. (1969). *American Business Abroad.* New Haven: Yale University Press.

Knickerbocker, F.T. (1973). *Oligopolistic Reaction and Multinational Enterprise.* Cambridge: Harvard University Press.

Kogut, B. (1983). "Foreign Direct Investment as a Sequential Process." *In The Multinational Corporation in the 1980s,* edited by C.P. Kindleberger, and D. Audretsch. Cambridge: The MIT Press.

Kudrle, R.T. (1991). "Several Faces of the Multinational Corporation: Political Reactions and Policy Response." In *International Political Economy,* edited by K.W. Stiles, and T. Akaha. New York: HarperCollins.

Kumazawa, M., and J. Yamada. (1989). "Jobs and Skills Under the Lifelong Nenko Employment Practice." In *The Transformation of Work,* edited by S. Wood. London: Unwin Hyman.

Lenin, V.I. (1917). *Imperialism: The Highest Stage of Capitalism.* Moscow: Progress.

Lillrank, P., and N. Kano. (1989). *Continuous Improvement: Quality Control Circles in Japanese Industry.* Ann Arbor: University of Michigan, Center for Japanese Studies.

Luxemburg, R. (1913). *The Accumulation of Capital.* London: Routledge and Kegan Paul.

M.I.T.I. (1993). Survey of Japan's Foreign Investment, Tokyo.

———. (1995). Survey of Japan's Foreign Investment, Tokyo.

Miyai, J. (1995). "The Redesign of Japanese Management Systems and Practices." *APO Productivity Journal* (Summer): 131-155.

Monden, Y. (1983). *Toyota Production System: Practical Approach to Production Management.* Atlanta: Industrial Engineering and Management Press.

Morita, A. (1992). "A Moment for Japanese Management," *Japan-Echo* 119 (2): 1-35.

Nohara, H. (1985). "Technologies Electroniques et Gestion de la Main-d'oeuvre dans l'Industrie Japonaise," *Revue d'Economie Industrielle* 34 (4): 325-347.

Nomura, M. (1993). *The End of Toyotism: Recent Trend of a Japanese Automobile Company.* Okayama: Okai University.

Nurkse, R. (1972). "Causes and Effects of Capital Movements." *In International Investment,* edited by J.H. Dunning. London: Penguin.

Oakland, J.S. (1993). *Total Quality Management: The Route to Improving Performances.* Oxford: Butterworth-Heinemann.

Organization of Economic Cooperation and Development. (1998). *Asian Crisis.* Paris: OECD.

Ohno, T. (1933). *Toyota Production System.* Cambridge, MA: Productivity Press.

Ohlin, B. (1933). *Interregional and International Trade.* Cambridge: Harvard University Press.

Porter, M.E. (1990). *The Competitive Advantage of Nations.* New York: The Free Press.

Redher, R. (1994). "Saturn, Uddevalla and the Japanese Lean Systems: Paradoxical Prototypes for the Twenty-first Century," *International Journal for Human Resource Management* 15 (1): 1-31.

Sandberg, A. (1995). *Enriching Production: Perspectives on Volvo's Udevalla Plant as an Alternative to Lean Production.* Aldershot, UK: Avebury.

Sasaki, S. (1994). *Struggle against Toyotism.* Tokyo: Aichi Institute on Labour Problems, the Asian Pacific Trade Union Symposium.

Shimada, H. (1993). "Japanese Management of Auto-production in the United States: An Overview of Human Technology in International Labour Organization." In *Lean Production and Beyond,* Report no. 92-9014-477-7: 61-79. Geneva: ILO.

Shingo, S. (1981). *A Study of the Toyota Production System from an Industrial Engineering Viewpoint.* Cambridge, MA: Productivity Press.

———. (1985). *A Revolution in Manufacturing: The SMED System.* Cambridge, MA: Productivity Press.

Streeck, W. (1992). *Social Institutions and Economic Performances: Studies of Industrial Relations in Advanced Capitalist Economics.* London: Sage.

Sunkel, O. (1992). "Big Business and Dependencia," *Foreign Affairs* 50 (April): 517-531.

Suzaki, K. (1987). *The New Manufacturing Challenge.* New York: The Free Press.

Tanaka, H. (1993). "Overseas Direct Investments and Trade," *Ex-Im Review* 13 (1): 27-93.

UNCTC. (1991). Government Policies and Foreign Direct Investment, Study no. A17. New York, NY.

Vernon, R. (1966). "International Investment and International Trade in the Product Cycle." *Quarterly Journal of Economics* 80: 190-207.

Wickens, P. (1987). *The Road to Nissan.* Basingstoke, UK: Macmillan Press.

Womack, J.P, D.T. Jones, and D. Rees. (1990). *The Machine that Changed the World.* New York: Rawson Associates.

World Bank. (1998). *Asian Economic Crisis.* Washington, DC: World Bank.

Yasuhara, N, K. Nishimura, S. Takada, and Y. Ogawa. (1995). "International Capital Flows in Recent Years," *Ex-Im Review* 15 (1): 1-67.

INDEX

ABOUT THE AUTHORS

Dipak R. Basu is a Professor of international economics at Nagasaki University, Japan. He has done research at Birmingham University and Cambridge University, England and was a lecturer at the Oxford University Institute of Agricultural Economics for several years. Presently, he is doing research on income distribution and growth with Irma Adelman of the University of California, Berkeley. Previously, he did research with Thomas Kronsjo of Birmingham University on optimal control system modelings in economics. He has published widely in major journals on system analysis, economics, and econometrics, and has presented papers at conferences of the Econometric Society, the Institute of Management Sciences, and the International Federation of Operations Research Societies. He is the author of *Future Energy Policies for the UK*, *Monetary and Financial Planning for a Transitory Economy*, and coauthor of *Energy Strategies for the UK*.

Victoria Miroshnik is working on a PhD in organizational behavior at the University of Queensland, Australia. She obtained her MS in psychology from Moscow State University, and MBA from Tiffin University, Ohio. She was awarded scholarships as an Outstanding Student in Georgia and Russia. She was a lecturer at Georgia State University in Tbilisi and consultant-psychologist for the Ministry of Defense of the Republic of Georgia. She worked for several years in corporate management and voluntary organizations in Russia. She has published a number of papers in international management journals. Her major areas of research are strategic management of multinational companies and organizational psychology.